Contents

Acknowledgments

We wish to publicly thank Mrs. Sue Clark of the great Paper City, more commonly known as Holyoke, Massachusetts, for her editing assistance. We want our readers to know that she is a consummate professional who has willingly volunteered her time and expertise helping us polish this book to make it more presentable and accessible to all. Mrs. Clark, please know that we are indebted to you for your contributions and ongoing support. This book is much improved because of your efforts.

Introduction

From Floundering to Fluent: Reaching and Teaching Struggling Readers was written for educational practitioners and specialists, particularly classroom teachers and school administrators, as well as family and community members, who are firmly committed to the reading development and academic success of all students, but particularly those who struggle with the act of reading. This book primarily focuses on gaining a deeper understanding of the kinds of difficulties that can attend the reading process, especially for at-risk readers and those with reading disabilities.

The various chapter authors address the myriad aspects of becoming a successful reader, including decoding, fluency, comprehension, and motivation to read. The book emphasizes the opportunities for all students to become solid readers and stresses that the act of reading must take place beyond the classroom doors. Strategies for engaging peers, family, and community in supporting struggling readers as they transition to skillful ones are embedded throughout the chapters, with the hopes that all who care about literacy as a key to unlocking a lifetime of knowledge and recreational pleasure will be encouraged to take part in this mission.

The motivation for writing this book comes from several concerns:

Our belief that reading is the fundamental tool to academic success;

Our awareness that approximately ten million children in this country have difficulty reading and of those struggling readers 90–95 percent can be helped to become proficient with early, effective intervention;

Our knowledge that experts report that students with a formal diagnosis of a reading disability comprise at least 20 percent of the population, but that only about 4 percent of school-aged students receive special education services for reading disabilities;

Our commitment to encouraging all students to see the value and pleasure of the multiple kinds of "nonacademic" reading;

Our understanding that reading quality literature plays a powerful role in positive human development;

Our belief that efforts to encourage reading in all students must extend beyond the classroom door and involve peers, family members, institutions, and community members;

Our years of experience in educating parents, teachers, school counselors, and other helping professionals that has led to the recognition that there is specific knowledge that could assist them in helping struggling readers become more proficient and involved readers; and

Our interest in identifying and sharing best practices that lead to reading success for those at risk of not being fluent, engaged readers.

We chose the first part of the title, *From Floundering to Fluent*, to highlight the journey that struggling readers can take, with the proper assistance. Many students struggle with reading, but are not formally diagnosed as having a reading disability. This can be due to different factors—requiring more time to master skills, needing specialized instruction in one or more subskills of reading, or having received poor instruction in earlier learning experiences. There are also students who have been formally diagnosed with a reading disability; reading-related supports and services can be written into their Individualized Education Plans. For these students, as with all struggling readers, socio-emotional problems such as shame, anxiety, or low self-esteem may accompany their wrestling with the act of reading.

Sociocultural and economic factors can threaten reading achievement. Too many children grow up in homes without a focus on literacy and language; such homes may lack books or role models who read. For many families, survival is more pressing than the luxury of literature. Language barriers may be present. For boys in this society, reading—or academic achievement, for that matter—may not be seen as "cool." Chosen texts and assigned readings may not seem relevant in that the characters, plots, settings or dilemmas do not resonate with young readers' lives and experiences. Additionally, technology may make reading seem slow, arduous, and outdated.

As students navigate their school years, they are presented with many developmental challenges and transitions. Reading can help them solve their critical issues and developmental crises through seeing how others in literature—true and fictitious characters—faced their own turning points and prevailed. Problem solving, forming a worldview, clarifying one's values, and empathizing with others are all products of reading quality literature. The more widely and frequently young people read, the more they enter worlds beyond their own. But ensuring a generation of fluent readers requires school, community, and family involvement.

The issues noted previously are the focal points of the chapters within this book. We try to balance theory, research, and proven best practices as we address the challenges that struggling readers confront and the strategies that may best assist them. This book, written by a team of veteran practitioners and scholars, takes a multipronged approach in that it covers the academic, socio-emotional, sociocultural, and personal components of reading.

We hope to stress that, while the number of struggling readers in our country is high, there are creative, proven approaches to address this problem. Like other practitioner-oriented sources, this book, where appropriate to the respective chapter, will provide a condensed review of the seminal literature, with suggestions to enhance practice. It is our belief that all who engage in the education and development of this nation's students will glean useful strategies to promote and strengthen their reading skills, attitudes, and habits.

Chapter One

Wrestling with Reading

*Understanding the Basics of Reading Disorders and
Associated Challenges*

Nicholas D. Young and Christine N. Michael

While "learning disabilities" (LD) is the umbrella term under which a number of specific disabilities fall, it is important that those interested in supporting struggling readers understand the ways in which students may experience reading disabilities themselves. Kilpatrick (2015) likens the situation to "the unfair race." This author asks us to picture a high school track meet in which there are six lanes on the track, four set up with no hurdles, one with high hurdles, and one with low hurdles. After the gun goes off, the runners race, with the runners in the two lanes with hurdles getting further and further behind.

He then describes the parallel with the development of reading skills among K–12 students, with the two-thirds who have no hindrances getting further and further ahead, and the other two lanes representing the estimated 30–34 percent of fourth graders who read below a basic level (Kilpatrick, 2015). As the gap between proficient and struggling readers widens, there are ancillary issues that can plague poor readers.

Virtually all current K–12 curricula and assessments require content reading skills. Poor reading skills can limit students' postsecondary and vocational options. Struggling readers are more likely to display behavioral problems in school and are at higher risk for depression. Students who were below reading level as early as third grade were four times more likely to become high school dropouts compared to proficient readers (Kilpatrick, 2015).

DEFINING LEARNING DISABILITIES

Before one can help a child or adolescent who is wrestling with reading problems, it is essential to have a foundational understanding of what learning disabilities are and, specifically, how learning disabilities can manifest themselves as specific reading disorders.

A simple definition is that learning disabilities are neurologically based processing problems. These problems can hinder a child's learning basic reading, writing, and/or math skills. Such problems also can impede higher-level skills such as organization, time planning, abstract reasoning, long-or short-term memory, and attention. Learning disabilities can affect an individual's life far beyond school and can interfere with relationships with family and friends and in the workplace.

The State of Learning Disabilities report (National Center for Learning Disabilities, 2014) states that learning disabilities "are not caused by visual, hearing or motor disabilities, intellectual disabilities (formerly referred to as mental retardation), emotional disturbance, cultural factors, limited English proficiency, environmental or economic disadvantages, or inadequate instruction" (p. 3). Estimates are that about 5 percent of the school-aged population (2.4 million) has some sort of learning disability. Two-thirds of students identified with learning disabilities are male, and Black and Hispanic students are overrepresented in many states.

The same report defines learning disabilities as "unexpected, significant difficulties in academic achievement and related areas of learning and behavior in individuals who have not responded to high-quality instruction and for whom struggle cannot be attributed to medical, educational, environmental or psychiatric causes" (p. 3). On the whole, people with learning disabilities are generally of average or above average intelligence, with a noticeable gap between their potential and actual achievement.

Some refer to learning disabilities as "hidden disabilities" or "invisible disabilities" as, on the surface, an individual may appear to be perfectly typical and seems to be very bright and intelligent, however, he or she may not be able to demonstrate the skill level expected from someone of a similar age. Most commonly, learning disabilities appear in a school-based setting and are diagnosed during the school years.

There are many instances, however, in which such problems go undiagnosed until college or even the adult years. In these cases, individuals are left to question why they struggle academically and socially. While there is no "cure" for a learning disability, with accurate evaluation, support, and intervention strategies, learning disabled individuals can achieve great success in all aspects of their lives.

UNDERSTANDING THE READING PROCESS

According to Sousa (2016, p. 93), there are three phases of learning to read. He states that "in the simplest terms, learning to read involves connecting two cerebral capacities that are already present in young brains: the spoken language networks with the visual recognition circuits." The first of the three phases is a pictorial stage in which a child's brain "photographs" words and visually "adjusts to the shape of the alphabet's letters." The second is the phonological stage where children begin decoding "letters (graphemes) into sounds (phonemes)." Finally, there is the orthographic stage in which children should be able to recognize words quickly and accurately.

Each phase activates different brain circuits; over time and with repetition, the circuits converge in a specialized area of the left hemisphere (the visual word form area). Successful reading involves the operations of decoding and comprehension. Children must learn that speech is composed of individual sounds, called phonemes, and that written spellings represent those sounds (the alphabetic principle). Early readers also must learn that the phonemes of spoken language can be reordered or recombined to form new words or rhymes. This permits the child to associate letters with sounds to build words and read; this is an early predictor of reading success (Sousa, 2016).

To read, one's brain must memorize the alphabet and which symbols (graphemes) correspond to the phonemes that are stored in his or her mental lexicon. Beginning readers must have phonemic awareness—that is, the understanding that written spellings represent sounds and that this combination applies phonics to the reading and spelling of words. Eventually, successful readers' brains learn to connect the twenty-six letters of the alphabet with the forty-four identified sounds of the spoken English language. Unfortunately for some readers, English is one of the most complex languages to master. As Sousa (2016) notes, "Because of the complexity of English orthography, there are more than 1,100 ways to spell the sounds of the 44-plus phonemes in English" (p. 96).

In the 1990s the National Institutes of Health used brain imaging to watch the activity of the three brain regions in the left hemisphere during the act of reading. The three brain centers work in concert to process the phoneme, map the connection between it and the letters that represent it, and then store the information in one's memory. When a student has learned a word, it becomes recognized automatically (National Institutes of Health [NIH], 2010). The automatic recognition center steps up its activity as readers become more and more skilled; however, while the aforementioned skills are required to learn to read, they are not all that is needed to read for meaning.

Children must also develop vocabulary and become able to easily grasp larger units of print (syllable patterns, whole words, and phrases). Ultimately, readers need to develop enough fluency in the reading process to be able to read for understanding (comprehension). Comprehension includes both a literal understanding of what one reads and, later, more reflective and advanced understandings, such as the ability to discern an author's point of view or bias (Sousa, 2016).

UNDERSTANDING READING DISABILITIES

Between 5 percent and 17 percent of children have reading disabilities (McCandliss & Noble, 2003). Links exist between reading disorders and delays in expressive language, receptive language, or both (Bidwell, 2016; Sousa, 2016). Because of this, children with reading disorders often are said to have a language-based learning disability.

There are three primary subtypes of reading disabilities that may or may not coexist
(Moats & Tolman, 2009). They are:

1. Phonological deficit, implicating a core problem in the phonological processing system of oral language
2. Processing speed/orthographic processing deficit, affecting speed and accuracy of printed word recognition (also called naming-speed problem or fluency problem)
3. Comprehension deficit, often coinciding with the first two types of problems, but specifically found in children with social-linguistic disabilities (e.g., autism spectrum), vocabulary weaknesses, generalized language learning disorders, and learning difficulties that affect "reading impaired" children (those who score below the 30th percentile in basic reading skills) (Moats & Tolman, 2009)

"Dyslexia" is the most commonly heard term related to reading problems and, over the years, there have been various definitions offered for the term. These definitions share the fact that dyslexic students struggle with reading and spelling. But it is important to know that no two dyslexic individuals have exactly the same assets and deficits when it comes to the reading process.

The term "dyslexia" was coined at the beginning of the twentieth century, when it was believed that it emanated from deficits in visual processing, with words and letters commonly being reversed and transposed. According to Eastwood (2016), it was invented by German ophthalmologist Rudolph Berlin, and comes from the Greek words *dys* (difficult) and *lexia* (reading). The term now refers to a spectrum of conditions that negatively affect reading ability; thus, reading disability and dyslexia are terms that, for the most part, can be used interchangeably.

The basic characteristic of a reading disorder is an impaired ability to read. Interestingly, brain scans show "atypical electrical activity in certain areas of the dyslexic brain when reading is happening (compared with the nondyslexic reader) but this varies from one dyslexic brain to another" (Bidwell, 2016, p. 41). Dyslexia has also been found to have a genetic basis and generally runs in families (Bidwell, 2016).

Phonological Processing

According to Vargo, Young, and Judah (2015), most students who wrestle with reading have a phonological processing disability. They describe phonemes as the most minute units of sound that can be used to produce speech. In a process that we humans are not consciously aware of, the brain breaks down words into these tiny units before we can recognize, understand, or remember them. The National Institutes of Health (2010) found that they could identify forty phonemes in the English language; that number has been increased to forty-four or more. Tests of children's ability with phonemes was a good predictor of later reading ability (NIH, 2010).

Phonological awareness is the ability to hear and understand the sound symbols that correspond to the words on a printed page, which is a critical component of early reading development. Bidwell (2016) writes that a student must have the ability "to hear and tell the difference between sounds made by different letters of the alphabet. They need to tell if two words rhyme or sound different. They need to be able to hear and distinguish the first, middle and end sounds within a word" (p. 43). Until phonological awareness is well developed, children cannot be expected to blend letter sounds together or segment the sounds in words.

In the 1990s the National Institutes of Health used brain imaging to watch the activity of the three brain regions in the left hemisphere during the act of reading. The three brain centers work in concert to process the phoneme, map the connection between it and the letters that represent it, and then store the information in one's memory. When a student has learned a word, it becomes recognized automatically (NIH, 2010).

For struggling readers, accessing the automatic recognition center is harder, so they must rely on the processing and mapping centers when figuring out words that they see. Their process, because it is not automatic, is slower and exacts more energy from them (NIH, 2010).

A grapheme is the smallest unit of written language, and it is essentially the use of visual symbols to represent spoken sounds, or phonemes. Reading requires the reader to recognize the visual sequence of letters in a certain order and pair it with the correct phonology. Students with impaired phonological awareness cannot effectively associate the visually processed letters with their proper sounds (Vargo, Young, & Judah, 2015).

Poor phonological awareness also causes other problems. Readers who suffer from this are also more likely to transpose sounds in words. They tend to mispronounce words more than their age peers. And they may have a difficult time or lack of interest in typical childhood activities such as learning a nursery rhyme or playing the game "I Spy" because of their struggles (Bidwell, 2016).

Characteristics of Fluency

Fluent reading requires the reader to avoid sounding out each word he or she encounters, but, instead, to sequentially scan the words and immediately recognize (read) them. Without fluency, the reading process slows to a halt. Fluent readers, naturally, must decode words that are foreign to them but eventually, through repetition, they store those new words in their memory. Through retrieval of the stored visual memory of the words, the reader is able to read automatically.

For some readers, working memory problems hamper their word reading skills (Kilpatrick, 2015). Working memory problems abound in children with learning disabilities of all types. As Sousa (2016) explains, skilled reading requires that readers "can retain verbal bits of information (phonemes) in working memory. Recent studies have shown distinct deficits among poor readers in this component of working memory, called phonological memory" (p. 103).

Sousa (2016) notes that the difficulties are most often seen in serial tasks, where the reader must hold on to a string of phonemes to form a word, or a string of words to make a sentence. Working memory plays a large role in integrating information while the reader is attempting to comprehend text and is critical to moderating overall outcomes in text comprehension (Jennings, Caldwell, & Lerner, 2013). The good news is that this can be a maturational delay in some students, who will outgrow the problem as they develop.

Processing Speed Issues

Ten to fifteen percent of poor readers will suffer from a different problem: they are accurate but are extremely slow in recognizing words and reading text. It is interesting to note that such readers perform relatively well on tests of phoneme awareness and other phonological skills. They do not easily or automatically recognize words and their spelling tends to be phonetic but not accurate.

Vargo, Young, and Judah (2015) point out that there is disagreement among professionals as to this problem; while some argue that this is essentially a timing or processing speed issue, others see this as a specific deficit within the orthographic processor that affects the storage and recall of exact letter sequences. As the authors note, these struggling readers' problems are generally less acute than those of students with phonological processing deficits.

If a student has a prominent and specific weakness in either phonological or rapid naming processing, he or she is labeled as having a single deficit in word recognition. If a student has a combination of phonological and naming-speed deficits, he or she possesses a double deficit (Kilpatrick, 2016). There are more double-deficit than single-deficit children, and thus, usually more difficult to remediate, although not always (Kilpatrick, 2016).

Children with reading disabilities often demonstrate a plethora of issues. Among them are attention problems, faulty pencil grip, poor letter formation, and anxiety. Additional deficits include weak impulse control, distractibility, task avoidance, difficulties comprehending spoken language, and confusion of mathematical signs and computational processes (Moats & Tolman, 2009).

Problems with Reading Comprehension

Ten to fifteen percent of poor readers can decode words better than they can understand the meanings of what they are reading. Unlike dyslexic poor readers, they can read words accurately and rapidly; they also can spell. Disorders of social reasoning, abstract verbal reasoning, or language comprehension lie at the root of the struggle (Moats & Tolman, 2009).

The National Association of Special Education Teachers (National Association of Special Education Teachers [NASET], n.d.) speaks of these readers in this way: "Some students with reading comprehension difficulties are able to read a passage so fluently you might assume they were highly proficient readers. However, when asked questions about what they have read, they have little or no understanding of the words" (p. 5). They are given the name "word callers" because of this condition.

Bidwell (2016) offers another explanation: "It may be that the child is still putting so much effort into decoding unknown words that there is little 'brain space' for her to think about what it all means" (p. 239). Poor working memory, as described earlier, may also be a root of comprehension problems (Kilpatrick, 2015; Bidwell, 2016; Sousa, 2016).

Deficits in reading comprehension show up as problems in understanding the seminal ideas in reading assignments. Comprehension problems may be expressed in problems in one or more of the following features: main idea identification; recall of sequential facts; or drawing inferences or interpreting the reading material (Bidwell, 2016). As a student moves into the upper grades, comprehension issues become more visible, as tasks involving reading are centered on academic content among the various subjects.

ASSETS AMONG DISORDERS

Sousa (2016) points out that "although dyslexia certainly causes reading difficulties and other learning challenges, it may also impart some cognitive strengths that scientists are beginning to explore" (p. 116). There is a higher incidence of dyslexia among successful entrepreneurs; dyslexics have sharper peripheral vision than others and "can give their attention to multiple auditory inputs at once" (p. 116). Other studies seem to show that dyslexia sharpens one's ability to recognize complex visual images and recognizing whether one has seen those images before.

Sousa (2016) describes the results of these studies as literally showing that dyslexic people can "see the big picture" more readily than the nondyslexic population. They may not be adept at focusing their attention as intently as others, which is a hallmark of skilled readers, who must shut out awareness of their surroundings in order to focus on reading. However, this lack of focus may make dyslexic students more globally aware and able to see big-picture details.

Such information is useful in intervention and in career choice.

OTHER ISSUES RELATED TO READING
COMPREHENSION DEFICITS

Nonlinguistic Factors

There are some other possible factors that cause unimpaired individuals to struggle mightily with the reading process. These include problems with perceiving sequential sounds (the inability to detect and discriminate among sounds presented in rapid sequence), sound frequency discrimination (inability to hear differences in sound frequency and discriminate tone and pitch in speech), and detection of target sounds in noises (difficulty discriminating between specific phoneme sounds and background noise) (Sousa, 2016). Any impairment to auditory acuity has the potential to affect reading (Jennings, Caldwell, & Lerner, 2013).

A child may also experience visual perceptual deficits in functional areas such as tracking and scanning, which can impede comprehension of text. As with hearing deficits, visual problems may have an impact on reading ability, although the relationship between reading and vision is a complex one. Two individuals with the same visual problem may experience it as either having an impact or no effect on reading effectively (Jennings, Caldwell, & Jenner, 2013).

In many cases, readers with any of these factors may fatigue, lose interest, or lose motivation due to the extra effort needed to read efficiently.

Emotional and Behavioral Issues

Reading problems can cause emotional and behavioral difficulty, and emotional and behavioral problems can hamper reading success. In both equations, the distractions caused by deficits in these different domains put a child at risk for diminished success. Morgan, Farkas, Tufis, and Sperling (2008) found that reading problems indeed elevated a child's odds of engaging in problem behaviors. Specifically, they found that, after statistically controlling for prior problem behavior, poor attention, and both SES- and demographic-related confounds, poor reading ability in first grade consistently acted as a statistically and clinically significant predictor of problem behavior in third grade.

In this same study, it was discovered that the odds of displaying poor task engagement, poor self-control, externalizing problem behaviors, or internalizing problem behaviors in third grade were 2.17, 1.33, 1.39, and 1.66 times higher, respectively, for poor readers than for average-to-good readers. The researchers also reported that poor readers in first grade were almost always poor readers in third grade. These odds were an extraordinary high 12.01 to 1.

Poor readers will often lose the motivation to do well in school. As failure becomes more prevalent, they will begin to adopt a more external locus of control, believing that no matter what they do, they are powerless to change their fate. They may express the belief that their successes or failures are dictated by luck, rather than their own internal factors such as hard work, dedication, or determination to succeed (NASET, n.d.).

Outwardly disruptive actions, then, are not the only behavioral or emotional challenges to positive achievement and social adaptation. Children with internalized disorders such as anxiety, depression, and social withdrawal are often too hampered by their emotional states to become active participants in the learning process or in social engagement. Poor readers with what Seligman (1992) termed "learned helplessness" may simply give up on tasks, even when success is possible, and withdraw into a self-defeating attitude of seeing their efforts in academic and social arenas as meaningless.

Attention Deficit/Hyperactivity Disorder (ADHD)

According to the National Institute of Mental Health (2016), attention-deficit/hyperactivity disorder (ADHD) is a brain disorder that is characterized by an ongoing pattern of inattention and/or hyperactivity-impulsivity; these characteristics interfere with normal functioning or development.

Children with ADHD often are assumed to have reading disorders as well, but this is not always true. ADHD and dyslexia are different disorders and may or may not overlap. While it is difficult to pinpoint how many students with ADHD also have dyslexia, the accepted range at this time falls between 18 and 40 percent (Sousa, 2016).

Social and Cultural Elements of Reading Problems

There is a rapid increase in the number of students in our schools who come from diverse cultural and linguistic backgrounds. English language learners are not initially proficient in the English language and may live in bilingual or multilingual households where other family members speak different languages (Jennings, Caldwell, & Lerner, 2013). When children's native dialect or language is different from what is being taught in school, they may struggle in ways that appear to be (but are not) similar to impediments caused by physiological deficits. As Sousa (2016) explains: "They come to school with a mental lexicon whose word representations often do not match what they are trying to decode on the printed page" (p. 99).

Genetics and Gender

Nationally, about three times as many boys as girls are identified with a reading disorder.

There is debate as to whether this is due to genetic deficits or other factors. Beaman, Wheldall, and Kemp (2006) question whether boys' classroom behavior, which tends to be more physical and rambunctious when compared to girls', may be to blame for an overly high classification. There also are questions about whether girls are underrepresented.

Quinn and Wagner's (2013) study of five hundred thousand beginning-second-grade students found the poor readers' ratio to be 1.6 to 1 for decoding and 2.4 to 1 for fluency (boy-to-girl ratio). But fascinatingly, only one in seven girls found to be reading impaired by the researchers had been classified with a reading disability by the school, suggesting that girls may be overlooked when it comes to reading problems. Yet another hypothesis is that elementary teachers tend to confound reading and handwriting competencies. Sousa (2016) points out that boys have significantly poorer writing skills but generally are almost as skilled as girls when it comes to early reading.

As far as genetics' role in dyslexia, there long have been associations between the condition and genetic mutations in twins and families (Sousa, 2016). More sophisticated research has been able to identify a half dozen of the specific genes involved. It appears that genetic mutations interfere with the movement of neurons in the fetal brain to their proper areas in the cortex, instead directing them to accumulate in tangles, most frequently in the visual word form area. This tangling stops the brain area from its normal functions of recognizing and decoding written text, so that the brain must construct other, inefficient pathways to complete the tasks (Kere, 2014; Platt et al., 2013).

Home and Environmental Literacy Factors

Home and environmental factors play a critical role in children's emotional and intellectual development; under the best conditions, home can be a solid foundation for deep and rapid cognitive, social, and emotional growth—all of which play parts in literacy development (Jennings, Caldwell, & Lerner, 2013).

Sadly, many of this country's children grow up in environments that are devoid of books, other reading materials, time, or other resources to devote to early literacy development. But families and communities can play a critical role in improving the experiences of struggling readers. As Bidwell (2016) notes, parents and caregivers do not need specific training to promote language and reading development, even among very young children.

Simple activities such as rhyming, word games, and even extended conversations help children become familiar with the sound systems of the English language. Magnetic letters and other manipulatives are valuable, as are trips to the library, having reading materials in the home, and the simple act of reading aloud, in paired reading sessions, or listening to children read on a regular basis (Bidwell, 2016). Familial attitudes toward the value of language and literacy shape children's own values and practices, so modeling reading and stressing the myriad ways that reading is used in daily life are essential elements in supporting young readers.

Parents' beliefs that even struggling readers can and will learn to read well are essential in building children's self-esteem and resiliency in the face of literacy challenges. Unfortunately, 2013 research on the parents of children with learning and attention issues (as cited in National Center for Learning Disabilities, 2014) found that 66 percent of parents were either "deeply struggling" or admitted to having "conflicted feelings" about their child's learning issues and their ability to help them. Additionally, they experienced serious stress and worry over their child's future.

EXTERNAL RISK FACTORS

Far too many American children come from increasingly risk-prone home environments that raise the chances of academic failure, including literacy.

The U.S. Census Bureau (2012) estimates that any particular night can see more than a half million children homeless. Poverty, family instability, homelessness, food instability, and violence within and outside the home all tax family and child well-being.

Children who are hungry, homeless, abused or neglected, or fearful or hypervigilant because of environmental factors come to school less able to focus on the academic and social tasks at hand; their families are equally taxed with stressors and also may be undereducated themselves. Children in such settings also are more prone to developmental issues that are the result of poor or nonexistent prenatal care (Jennings, Caldwell, & Lerner, 2013).

Besides the aforementioned factors, the sad truth is that many children whose lives are affected by risk factors also are forced to attend the poorest and most unstable schools. In the poorest neighborhoods, students generally have the least-prepared teachers, the most turnover in teaching staff and leadership, and the least safe environments surrounding school settings.

A 2015 ACT Learning Policy Institute report demonstrates that teachers in Title 1 schools leave at a 50 percent higher rate than other teachers; teachers in high-poverty, high-minority schools leave at an even higher rate; and teachers of color, 75 percent of whom work in high-poverty schools, leave at the highest rates; such instability can wreak havoc with consistent educational practice.

INTERVENTIONS AND SUPPORTS

Three federal laws protect the rights of children and adults with learning disabilities and ensure that all individuals receive the special education services that they need, as well as equitable treatment in schools and the workplace. Section 504 of the Rehabilitation Act of 1973 does not fund specific programs to support individuals with disabilities, but it does prohibit discrimination in federally funded activities and programs; thus, students with LD who need only reasonable accommodations or modifications to their educational programs to be successful are served under Section 504. All students eligible for IDEA supports (see next paragraph) are also eligible under Section 504 (National Center for Learning Disabilities, 2014).

The first is the Individuals with Disabilities Education Act (IDEA), passed in 1975 (U.S. Department of Education, 2004). This early legislation provides special education and its related services to youth aged three to twenty-one. Children with any one of thirteen handicapping conditions, including specific learning disabilities such as dyslexia, are entitled to a free and appropriate education delivered in the least restrictive environment. The act also provides transitioning planning help (National Center for Learning Disabilities, 2014).

IDEA is joined by the Americans with Disabilities Act (ADA), which was amended in 2008. The primary focus of this act protects individuals who have physical or mental impairments that restrict one or more major life activities; "learning" is considered one such life activity. Individuals with learning disabilities are protected from discrimination in educational and work settings, and are afforded reasonable accommodations to allow them to succeed in the workplace (National Center for Learning Disabilities, 2014).

More recently, IDEA was strengthened to include significant elements that relate to literacy instruction. Most notable is the response to intervention (RTI) model, which is a data-driven process of decision making. It includes early identification and the implementation of evidence-based and research-proven strategies. The beauty of RTI is that it begins with "high-quality instruction and universal screening of all children in the general education classroom and provides struggling learners with interventions at increasing levels of intensity to accelerate their rate of learning" (National Center for Learning Disabilities, 2014, p. 14).

Now, schools are able to implement appropriate, evidence-based intervention and remediation before a student falls too far below grade level and before being deemed eligible for special education services. Departing from the earlier "discrepancy model," RTI can provide a variety of services, provided by diverse personnel (general education teachers, special educators, and specialists), with each student's progress being closely monitored as to both individual rate of learning and level of performance (National Center on Response to Intervention, 2010).

The Home Factor

Although explored later in this book in greater detail, the home factor (as well as community supports) can play a huge role in helping struggling readers gain mastery and pleasure in reading. Chapter 8, "Beyond the Schoolhouse Door," specifically addresses ways in which a child's family and community can play a powerful role in promoting literacy and bolstering the efforts of school-based reading efforts.

CONCLUSION

As many as 5 percent of American school children (2.4 million) have a learning disability, and reading disabilities are prevalent among them. Up to 10 percent of people suffer reading difficulties, and most are of average or above average intelligence. Historically, reading disabilities have been referred to as "dyslexia," and they are specific learning disabilities that are displayed in severe deficits in the reading process. These deficits affect other areas of development, such as language and functioning.

Of all reading disabilities, phonological processing deficiencies are most common. Early readers with these deficiencies suffer impaired abilities in their abilities to hear, discriminate, recognize, and understand the various sound components in language. Struggling readers may also have impaired phonological awareness—the ability to hear and understand the sound-symbol correspondences of the printed page. These deficiencies can hamper reading ability, fluency, and enjoyment if not addressed properly.

There are also social, cultural, and emotional factors that can help or hinder reading acquisition and fluency. These range from cultural differences, behavioral and social problems, the effects of poverty and family stress, and substandard schooling. The positive news is that skilled diagnosis, support, and intervention can mitigate the struggles of disabled readers. Educators, family members, and communities have critical roles to play in supporting all readers and developing each student's literacy capacity to its fullest so that the student can fulfill his or her potential in academic, social, community, and career functions.

POINTS TO REMEMBER

- The three main processes for understanding the written word are phonological processing, processing speed, and comprehension. Students who have a phonological processing disability comprise the largest group of struggling readers.
- Approximately 5 percent of school-aged children (2.4 million) have a learning disability and reading disabilities are prevalent among them. The primary characteristic of a reading disorder is an impaired ability to read.
- Reading achievement can be affected by social, cultural, and emotional factors in and out of the school setting. Struggling readers can be supported by family, school, and community efforts to promote and reward literacy.
- There are nonlinguistic causes of reading difficulty, including those in the auditory and visual domains. Gender and genetics play a role in dyslexia.
- Response to Intervention (RTI) is a multi-tiered approach to identifying students based on low achievement, application of certain criteria for exclusion, and response to varying levels of intervention.

REFERENCES

ACT Learning Policy Institute. (2015). *The condition of future educators.* Retrieved from www.act.org/content/dam/act/unsecured/documents/Future-Educators-2015.pdf

Beaman, R., Wheldall, K., & Kemp, C. (2006). Differential teacher attention to boys and girls in the classroom. *Educational Review, 58,* 339–366.

Bidwell, V. (2016). *The parents' guide to specific learning disabilities.* London: Jessica Kingsley.

Eastwood, N. (2016). *Psychology of reading and the brain.* Self-published. Retrieved from www.plutoscave.com.

Jennings, J. H., Caldwell, J. S., & Lerner, J. W. (2013). *Reading problems: Assessment and teaching strategies.* Saddle River, NJ: Pearson.

Kere, J. (2014). The molecular genetics and neurobiology of developmental dyslexia as model of a complex phenotype. *Biochemical and Biophysical Research Communications, 452*(2), 236–243.

Kilpatrick, D. A. (2015). *Essentials of assessing, preventing, and overcoming reading difficulties.* Hoboken, NJ: Wiley.

McCandliss, B. D., & Noble, K. G. (2003). The development of reading impairment: A cognitive neuroscience model. *Mental Retardation Developmental Disabilities Research Reviews, 19*(3), 196–204. doi:10.1002/mrdd.10080. PMID 12953299

Moats, L., & Tolman, C. (2009). *Language essentials for teachers of reading and spelling (LETRS): The challenge of learning to read (Module 1).* Boston, MA: Sopris West.

Morgan, P. L., Farkas, G., Tufis, P. A., & Sperling, R. A. (2008). Are reading and behavioral problems risk factors for each other? *Journal of Learning Disabilities, 41*(5), 417–436.

National Association of Special Education Teachers. (n.d.). *Characteristics of children with learning disabilities.* Retrieved from http://www.naset.org/fileadmin/user_upload/LD_Report/Issue__3_LD_Report_Character istic_of_LD.pdf

National Center for Learning Disabilities. (2014). *The state of learning disabilities.* Retrieved from www.ncld.org/wp-content/uploads/2014/11/2014-State-of-LD.pdf

National Center on Response to Intervention. (2010). *Essential components of RTI: A closer look at response to intervention.* Washington, DC: US Department of Education, Office of Special Education Programs.

National Institute of Mental Health. (2016). *Attention deficit disorder and ADHD.* Retrieved from https://www.nimh.nih.gov/health/topics/attention-deficit-hyperactivity-disorder-adhd/index.shtml

National Institutes of Health. (2010). *Fact sheet: Reading difficulty and disability.* Retrieved from https://report.nih.gov/NIHfactsheets/ViewFactSheet.aspx?csid=114

Platt, M. P., Adler, W. T., Melhorn, A. J., Johnson, G. C., Wright, K. A., Choi, R. T., & Rosen, G. D. (2013). Embryonic disruption of the candidate dyslexia susceptibility gene homolog Kiaa0319-like results in neuronal migration disorders. *Neuroscience,* 248,585593.

Quinn, J. M., & Wagner, R. K. (2013). Gender differences in reading impairment and in the identification of impaired readers: Results from a large-scale study of at-risk readers. *Journal of Learning Disabilities, 48*(4), 433–445.

Seligman, M. (1992). *Learned optimism.* New York, NY: Pocket Books.

Sousa, D. A. (2016). *How the special needs brain learns.* Thousand Oaks, CA: Corwin.

U.S. Census Bureau. (2012). *The Statistical Abstract of the United States: 2012.* Retrieved from https://www2.census.gov/library/publications/2011/compendia/statab/131ed/2012-statab.pdf

U.S. Department of Education. (2004). *Individuals with Disabilities Education Act.* Retrieved from http://idea.ed.gov/

Vargo, F. E., Young, N. D., & Judah, R. D. (2015). The fundamentals of reading disorders: Gaining insight into causes and effects. In N. D. Young & C. N. Michael (Eds.), *Beyond the bedtime story: Promoting reading development during the middle school years* (pp. 47–58). Lanham, MD: Rowman & Littlefield.

Chapter Two

Spotting Problems before They Grow

Preventing and Remediating Reading Difficulties for Elementary and Secondary Students

Jade Wexler, Jeanne Wanzek, and Sharon Vaughn

This chapter provides an overview of two primary approaches to addressing reading difficulties/disabilities: prevention and remediation. We first discuss issues related specifically to preventing and remediating reading difficulties for students at the elementary level and then, in the second half of the chapter, we describe issues and programs at the secondary level.

Prevention—in an educational setting—refers to a course of action designed to keep something from happening. In contrast, remediation is the act of correcting or remedying an existing problem. Thus, with respect to reading difficulties, prevention refers to instruction aimed at keeping a reading difficulty from occurring or becoming worse. Remediation is necessitated when a reading difficulty or disability has been identified and a significant course of action is required to improve reading performance.

Prevention and remediation are commonplace in the medical field. For example, preemptive measures such as exercise or low-salt diets are suggested as a means of preventing disease. These procedures are often "prescribed" when individuals are determined to be "at risk" for developing disease. Similarly, in reading, providing reading interventions (additional reading instruction) to students who may be at risk for developing reading difficulties is a preventative practice aimed at reducing the number of students with reading difficulties.

Prevention for reading difficulties is typically associated with the younger grades—preschool, kindergarten, and first and second grades—however, prevention can also be part of reading instruction for older students. As text and vocabulary demands increase, preventative instruction can assist students in effectively reading and comprehending more advanced content-area text.

Remediation in the medical field is the treatment provided to cure an existing, diagnosed disease. In most cases, treatment of disease is more successful when there is early diagnosis. When a reading difficulty is identified, remediation suggests an intensive intervention in order to "treat" the identified difficulty. As in medicine, early diagnosis of a reading difficulty may lead to more successful remediation because the student is not yet significantly behind. Although prevention and remediation at the elementary and secondary levels share some instructional similarities, there are also differences due to the distinctive needs of younger and older readers and the practical applicability of putting prevention and remediation efforts in place at the two levels.

In this chapter, we will review the literature on effective preventative and remedial interventions, identify the key components of these interventions, and provide steps for successfully implementing prevention and remediation for elementary and secondary students.

INTERVENTIONS IN THE ELEMENTARY GRADES

Essential Instruction

Research examining effective reading instruction for beginning readers provides essential guidance for instructional practice for elementary students (Foorman & Wanzek, 2016; National Early Literacy Panel, 2009; Wanzek et al., 2016). These syntheses and reports confer that explicit, integrated instruction in the components of reading including phonics and word recognition, fluency, language, and comprehension yield positive reading outcomes for many students.

The National Reading Panel report (2000), which has guided recent research and practice, specifically identified five critical components of reading instruction necessary for young readers to successfully gain reading skill and reach the ultimate goal of reading fluently and comprehending text: (a) phonological awareness, (b) phonics, (c) fluency, (d) vocabulary, and (e) comprehension. Effective elementary reading interventions including these components allow students to interact with text daily while developing the skills needed to read and comprehend the text.

Phonological Awareness

Phonological awareness refers to a student's ability to orally produce and manipulate individual sounds in spoken words. For example, if a teacher says the word "slip," a student can orally identify the sounds as /s/ /l/ /i/ /p/.

Students who are lacking in phonological awareness often struggle with reading. However, there is evidence that students with low phonological awareness can be taught the necessary skills (Blachman, 2000; Liberman & Shankweiler, 2013).

Analysis of the components of words (e.g., What are the sounds in the word "mat"? /m/ /a/ /t/) is a critical skill related to future reading development (National Early Literacy Panel, 2009). The strongest student outcomes are found when phonological awareness instruction is integrated with other foundational reading skills such as letter-sound correspondence and blending sounds for word reading (Liberman & Shankweiler, 2013; National Early Literacy Panel, 2009).

Phonics and Word Recognition

Phonics and word recognition are also foundational skills necessary for an elementary reader to effectively access print. Instruction in letter-sound correspondences, blending of letter sounds to decode words, and the use of rhymes to read families of words (e.g., the words "cat," "sat," "bat," and "mat" are built with the rhyme -at) all improve students' word recognition abilities (O'Connor, 2014; O'Shaughnessy & Swanson, 2000). More advanced word recognition instruction involves teaching larger graphophonic units such as letter combinations (e.g., ing, sh, ea) and morphemes (-ly, mono) and is associated with improved word recognition and comprehension abilities (Bowers, Kirby, & Deacon, 2010; Carlisle, 2010; Nunes, Bryant, & Barros, 2012).

Elementary interventions for students with reading difficulties include systematic phonics instruction where scaffolding can be used to build from the smaller, simpler units (e.g., letter sounds) to larger units and word parts (e.g., letter combinations, rhymes, affixes), providing students with specific skills for decoding increasingly complex words.

Fluency

Students with reading difficulties often struggle with fluency—reading text accurately and with adequate speed (Kim, Wagner, & Lopez, 2012; Lai, Benjamin, Schwanenflugel, & Kuhn, 2014). Affecting student outcomes in the area of fluency has proven to be a challenging task. For example, a meta-analysis of research on fluency interventions noted effect sizes of .47 for reading fluency interventions at posttest, but reduced to .28 approximately one year later (Suggate, 2016). Phonics and reading comprehension interventions had better long-term outcomes for students.

Nevertheless, fluency is a key component of reading. Students who read slowly without automaticity spend much of their effort on decoding words and may be unable to focus their attention on the meaning of the text. Generally, students who can read text fluently are better overall readers, demonstrating understanding of the text they read (Silverman, Speece, Harring, & Ritchey, 2013).

Research examining ways to improve students' fluency has reported instruction in reading fluently and setting goals for fluent reading is valuable for improving student achievement (Morgan, Sideridis, & Hua, 2012). Fluency instruction has been carried out successfully in a variety of ways. Practicing fluent reading with echo reading, repeated readings, wide reading of a range of texts, and peer or pair tutoring are successful strategies for increasing fluency on practiced text (Connor, Alberto, Compton, & O'Connor, 2014; Morgan et al., 2012).

Oral Language

Wide language and vocabulary knowledge is pertinent to effective comprehension of text (Elleman, Lindo, Morphy, & Compton, 2009; Kershaw & Schatschneider, 2012; Shany & Biemiller, 2010). Language and vocabulary refers to the words and structure students understand and use when listening, speaking, reading, and writing. Elementary students can advance in their language and vocabulary through direct and indirect experiences with oral and printed language. Indirect experiences that serve to increase student language and vocabulary include opportunities to engage in oral discussions of new experiences, concepts, and words that build on previous knowledge.

Explicit instruction of specific word meanings or language structure is also necessary to increase student exposure to novel words and language uses (Luftus, Coyne, McCoach, Zipoli, & Pullen, 2010; Stahl & Fairbanks, 2006; Tuckwiller, Pullen, & Coyne, 2010). Direct vocabulary instruction is most effective when words are selected and incorporated in text based on their usefulness in language and importance to comprehension (Beck, McKeown, & Kucan, 2002). Repeated exposure to new vocabulary in a variety of contexts is also vital to ensuring significant student reading gains (Beck & McKeown, 2007).

Comprehension

The ultimate goal of reading is to be able to comprehend the text. Phonological awareness, word recognition, fluency, and language and vocabulary are all necessary components of successful, meaningful reading leading to comprehension. Students demonstrating a mastery of skills in each of these areas are on the right track for successful reading. Students must also acquire specific comprehension practices and strategies to effectively gain meaning from different types of text (McKeown, Beck, & Blake, 2009).

Instructional techniques to improve reading comprehension in elementary interventions include teaching students to monitor their comprehension, generate questions about the text, organize and retell information presented, recognize text structures, predict outcomes in the text, and confirm or revise predictions (McLaughlin, 2012; National Reading Panel, 2000).

Prevention at the Elementary Level

Studies aimed at the prevention of reading difficulties often occur early (kindergarten and first grade) and as a result include explicit instruction on building prereading skills (phonemic awareness, phonics, oral vocabulary) and their basic application to the reading of words or understanding of text. The outcomes of these interventions demonstrate that many students can get on track for successful reading in foundational skills as well as in language/comprehension (Vellutino, Scanlon, & Jaccard, 2003; Wanzek et al., 2016).

As a result, prevention interventions have been shown to reduce the number of students who struggle with reading (Carney & Stiefel, 2008; O'Connor, Bocian, Beach, Sanchez, & Flynn, 2013; Wanzek & Vaughn, 2011). Multicomponent interventions with integration of instruction in several reading components can yield the strongest outcomes for students as they progress into the upper elementary grades (Wanzek, Wexler, Vaughn, & Ciullo, 2010).

To prevent reading difficulties from occurring in the elementary grades, early identification of students at risk for reading difficulties is key. A critical step is establishing school-wide screening and preventative intervention practices in kindergarten and first grade for identifying students at risk. What factors indicate a student is at risk for reading difficulties?

Risk in the reading field has typically been defined by reading or reading-related skills that predict future reading ability. Several early reading skills have shown potential as predictors of future reading ability. Students demonstrating difficulties in oral language, phonological processing, print concepts, letter knowledge, phonological awareness, and word decoding skills may be at risk for reading difficulties (Fuchs et al., 2012; National Early Literacy Panel, 2009). When a student has been identified as "at risk" for reading difficulties, preventative intervention may be warranted.

IMPLEMENTING PREVENTATIVE INTERVENTIONS IN THE ELEMENTARY GRADES

The first step in a prevention program for students with reading difficulties/disabilities is to identify and regularly use reliable and valid screening instruments to identify students at risk for reading difficulties. Though reviews of appropriate screening procedures are beyond the scope of this chapter, the website for the National Center on Response to Intervention (www. rti4success.org) provides an analysis of reliable and valid measures for early screening of reading difficulties.

The critical features of effective screening are: (a) the measure is reliable and valid; (b) the measure can be readily administered by school personnel without excessive training and knowledge for interpretation; (c) the measure does not allow for many false negatives—that is, students who are at risk are missed with the screening; and (d) the screening is available as early as kindergarten. After students who are "at risk" for reading difficulties are identified, prevention practices can be established to remedy difficulties and assure grade-level progress.

There are two goals of preventative intervention: (a) to assist students in getting on the right track with any identified "at-risk" skill areas and (b) to prevent students from struggling with more advanced reading skills. For example, a student demonstrating risk in the area of basic decoding or alphabetic principle may need targeted instruction in letter sounds and blending sounds to read words. A weakness in early decoding may also suggest the student will struggle with more advanced reading skills in the future. As a result, other grade-appropriate instruction, such as irregular word reading, vocabulary, and comprehension strategies, may be included in the intervention in order to prevent the student from falling behind in these areas.

The instructional focus of the intervention should be adjusted to meet student needs. A student struggling with many letter names and letter sounds may need to spend more time on letter-sound identification and less time on text reading because of the limited number of words the student can read. As the student progresses in letter-sound knowledge, the word reading and text reading instruction can be increased.

The intervention may also include more time on oral skills initially while gradually moving to more print-oriented skills. For example, students not yet reading words can still benefit from oral language and vocabulary instruction and listening comprehension instruction. As students progress in reading, the vocabulary and comprehension strategies previously taught orally can be transferred into reading vocabulary and reading comprehension.

Several foundational skills may be a part of a prevention intervention, including phonological awareness and phonics. These foundational skills can allow students to access meaningful reading such as reading words, sentences, and short passages (stories) and provide clear connections between instruction in the foundational skills and the act of reading text. The meaning of individual words (vocabulary) and sentences or passages (comprehension) can also be integrated in the instruction.

Once students begin the planned intervention, progress monitoring is essential to guide appropriate instructional decisions during the intervention (Fuchs & Fuchs, 2011). Student progress should be monitored in any areas where students have demonstrated below-grade-level performance on the screening measures.

A student who scores below expected outcomes on a screening measure of word reading would require targeted instruction to accelerate student learning in this area. Progress should be monitored to determine whether the intervention is improving student ability in word reading; if so, then the intervention is effective and instruction should continue until the student is on track. Should progress monitoring during the intervention indicate that the student is not making enough progress to achieve grade-level performance, then further instructional adjustments to intensify the intervention are needed to accelerate student progress.

Instructional adjustments can be made in two ways: (a) content of intervention and (b) delivery of instruction. The content refers to the actual skills students are taught; for example, a student struggling with word reading would require targeted instruction related to phonics, regular-word reading, irregular-word reading, word reading fluency, and applications of these word reading areas in text reading. Should the student continue to struggle with word reading after the intervention has begun, the content of the intervention can be examined to determine whether areas related to word reading (e.g., word reading fluency) are not currently being taught or may need more emphasis in the intervention.

Next, instructional delivery should be examined. If the necessary content and emphasis are addressed in the intervention and the student is still not making sufficient progress, there may be difficulties in the way the instruction is delivered. Adjusting instruction in these ways may improve student learning (Vaughn, Wanzek, Murray, & Roberts, 2012):

- Breaking instruction into smaller steps so that students can master them, linking the steps until students have mastered the skill
- Including more explicit instruction by modeling and overtly teaching each of the skills needed to complete the task
- Providing more opportunities to practice the new skills
- Adding concrete materials to make the instruction more explicit
- Providing immediate feedback to students during initial practice opportunities
- Providing extensive review of the skills being taught

Preventative intervention can be effective in improving student reading during the early grades. Interventions designed to prevent should be focused on improving student foundational skills, developing fluency in these skills, and explicitly teaching the application of these skills to reading and understanding text.

REMEDIATION AT THE ELEMENTARY LEVEL

Remediation of reading difficulties in the elementary grades typically occurs under three conditions: (a) when students demonstrate extensive difficulties with language and learning such that immediate and intensive intervention is warranted, (b) when students have participated in typically effective prevention programs and their performance continues to be lower than expected, and (c) when students have specific reading needs that prevent them from succeeding in their content courses—such as significant problems integrating multiple text types or summarizing key ideas.

How might teachers recognize that students' reading problems require remediation? Several indicators can be considered, including: (a) many errors in word reading when students are reading text at or below their grade level; (b) difficulty reading individual words in isolation or within text; (c) slow, labored reading of sentences or passages on their grade level or below; and (d) difficulty understanding the text—with special consideration for whether these comprehension problems persist even when students have adequate vocabulary and background knowledge for the topic they are reading.

Students demonstrating significant difficulties in one or more of the above areas may have a reading difficulty that requires remediation. Many reading difficulties are apparent early when text reading demands become commonplace. However, some reading difficulties may not surface until the upper elementary grades when text reading demands increase (e.g., length and complexity of text increase; reading to learn in the content areas is expected). Once a reading difficulty is identified, remediation is essential to assist the student in improving reading performance.

IMPLEMENTING REMEDIAL INTERVENTIONS IN THE ELEMENTARY GRADES

As with prevention, appropriate screening measures should be used to identify students with reading difficulties in need of remedial intervention. These measures may include assessments of oral reading fluency, word identification, and/or vocabulary and comprehension. The goal of remediation is to get students back on grade level in their reading. To meet this goal, instruction may include teaching foundational skills students have not yet mastered as well as grade-specific skills that will assist students in gaining the necessary reading skills to be successful.

Similar to preventative interventions, time allocations and skill areas to target within remedial interventions should be designed to meet student needs. Instruction may be targeted at the word reading level for a group of students struggling with these foundational skills. Time can be adjusted differently for students demonstrating basic accuracy in word reading but strug- gling with vocabulary and comprehension strategies. Remedial interventions must often be more "intense" than interventions designed to prevent reading difficulties in order to improve outcomes for students who continue to strug- gle with reading (Vaughn, Wexler et al., 2012).

How can the intensity of an intervention be increased? Decreasing group size for instruction is one way to increase intervention intensity and increase student outcomes. Smaller group sizes provide intensity in remediation be- cause instructional content can be targeted more closely to individual student needs. In addition, smaller groups may allow teachers to more specifically meet student needs with more explicit and systematic instruction and in- creased opportunities for student practice.

Increasing the amount of time students receive intervention may be a second way to increase the intensity of an intervention. Interventions in reading have typically been set between twenty and fifty minutes per day. One of the most intense interventions can be found in a study by Torgesen et al. (2001). In this study, eight- to ten-year-old students with reading disabil- ities were provided with a reading intervention for two fifty-minute sessions per day over eight to nine weeks. The 67.5 hours of instruction yielded substantial improvements in word reading and comprehension that were maintained over the next two years; thus, more time spent in intervention may benefit students with severe reading disabilities who are in need of remedial interventions.

Remedial interventions must target the high-impact skills in reading to accelerate student learning. Not all grade-level reading skills can be covered during an intervention (though all grade-level skills should be addressed sufficiently in the ongoing core reading instruction). For this reason, it is important to identify skills with the highest impact on reading that will allow the students to accelerate their learning, better access their core classroom reading instruction, and be successful with reading.

As with prevention, progress monitoring is essential for determining the impact of the intervention. To assist in determining whether the intervention is having the intended impact, it may be helpful to set short-term goals for student progress. For example, you may calculate the expected weekly gain on progress-monitoring measures in order to evaluate progress toward the overall goal of grade-level performance. The following formula can assist in determining short-term goals:

1. Grade-Level Goal – Student Score = Gain Needed
2. Gain Needed ÷ Number of Weeks Left in School Year = Weekly Goal

Monitoring student progress in relation to these short-term goals can help teachers determine the need for instructional adjustments. Providing intensive, remedial interventions that address the key components of reading can accelerate the reading progress of elementary students with severe reading difficulties. The focus of remediation should be on the areas where students are struggling as well as explicit strategies for independent reading.

INTERVENTIONS AT THE SECONDARY LEVEL

Secondary students face the demands of more difficult curricula and content as well as meeting rising national and state standards (National Governors Association Center for Best Practices & Council of Chief State School Officers, 2010; Next Generation Science Standards Lead States, 2013). Despite the students having a reading difficulty or disability, educators have expectations that they will be able to decode fluently and comprehend material with challenging content (Edmonds et al., 2009).

These expectations present challenges for all teachers, including general education content-area teachers, who must be well prepared to meet the needs of a variety of learners. In fact, students with disabilities currently spend a majority of their day in the general education content-area setting (Institute of Education Sciences [IES], National Center for Special Education Research, 2006).

Although we have an increasingly sophisticated knowledge base about how to implement effective interventions for most beginning readers, some students either fail to receive these interventions or do not respond adequately to them. Therefore, despite recent expectations that students will read and comprehend upper-level text and meet national and state standards, many students continue to struggle with reading in the upper grades.

The National Assessment of Educational Progress, or the Nation's Report Card, reveals data showing that more than 60 percent of eighth graders and 60 percent of twelfth graders scored below the proficient level in reading achievement (National Center for Education Statistics, 2015a, 2015b). For students of color, matters are even worse. In 2013, 17 percent of African American students and 22 percent of Hispanic students read at a proficient level. These students are most at risk for poor reading outcomes (ACT Inc., 2009, 2013).

Despite the low performance of many secondary level students, becoming a competent reader remains a crucial skill essential to individual and societal success (Biancarosa & Snow, 2006). When students continue to struggle with reading at the secondary level, several consequences can result, including, for example, an inability to graduate from high school and criminal justice system involvement (Hernandez, 2012).

Due to a combination of continued frustration and a lack of reading instruction, many secondary struggling readers read infrequently. In fact, authors of several studies at the secondary level have confirmed that middle and high school teachers, faced with pressure to cover a vast amount of curriculum with classes full of students who are struggling to read, often resort to circumventing the use of text all together (Swanson et al., 2015; Wexler, Mitchell, Clancy, & Silverman, 2016). These studies confirm that many teachers are not consistently integrating the use of text into their content-area instruction or providing instruction in strategies to support the use of text necessary for secondary students with reading difficulties and disabilities to make gains.

When students are not required to read often and/or not provided instruction in how to read complex text to access content, a phenomenon known as "the Matthew effect" (Stanovich, 1986) can occur; thus, as a result of reading less and not receiving explicit instruction in how to read and comprehend text, students may experience further regression in reading as well as in their vocabulary, background knowledge, and overall content acquisition. These are the very students who need us to implement prevention and remediation practices.

Before we can adequately design appropriate models to serve our students, we must further explore what exactly prevention and remediation entail at the secondary level and what the features of a prevention and remediation model might look like.

PREVENTION AT THE SECONDARY LEVEL

Prevention of reading difficulties at the secondary level may sound like an oxymoron. Is it possible for teachers to provide prevention in reading difficulties and disabilities for students who should already be able to read? If prevention includes the idea of preventing students from falling behind, isn't it too late to provide prevention and time instead to provide strong remedial intervention efforts for adolescent struggling readers? What types of students are in need of prevention? Who should implement interventions aimed at prevention? When should these interventions be implemented? These are just some of the questions that might come to mind when contemplating the idea of providing prevention at the secondary level.

Students in need of instruction aimed at prevention of reading difficulties and disabilities are those who struggle with comprehension, the ultimate goal of reading. Though these students demonstrate adequate foundational-level skills (e.g., word reading), as they progress into the upper grades and are faced with more challenging content-specific text, they frequently encounter difficulties reading and comprehending that text. The complex text at the upper grades that students encounter can be laden with unfamiliar text structure, confusing graphics, and challenging vocabulary (Gersten, Fuchs, Williams, & Baker, 2001; Sáenz & Fuchs, 2002).

Students may struggle for a variety of reasons, including poor vocabulary knowledge, limited background knowledge, limited knowledge and ability to apply fix-up strategies (e.g., main idea generation), and poor decoding ability of multisyllabic words. These students can benefit from direct instruction in key ideas and vocabulary prior to reading text and receiving instruction in strategies they can use to become independent learners. For these reasons, it is important to consider the processes needed when structuring and designing a prevention model.

IMPLEMENTING PREVENTATIVE INTERVENTIONS AT THE SECONDARY GRADES

Prevention techniques can be implemented school-wide across all general education content-area classes. After all, the goal of these efforts is to give students tools to help them be more successful at reading and comprehending text so that they can access content from that text. Ultimately, we hope that these practices will prevent students from falling behind and needing remediation. Therefore, considering that a majority of students in need of this instruction spend most of their day in the general education content-area setting, all content-area teachers should integrate instruction aimed at prevention into their content-area general education classes (Reed, Wexler, & Vaughn, 2012).

So, what are evidence-based prevention practices that content-area teachers can realistically implement to target students' needs? While some strategies can be considered unique to each discipline, such as content-specific vocabulary or reading maps in social studies (Heller & Greenleaf, 2007; Lee & Spratley, 2010; Shanahan & Shanahan, 2008), many strategies are appropriate for use across the content areas. Furthermore, we do not expect content-area teachers to teach the most foundational-level skills to their students (e.g., word reading). If students are in need of support in foundational-level skills, they are likely good candidates for remediation support, and this should occur during a supplemental remediation class by a reading specialist, described in the subsequent section.

Authors of several meta-analyses and reports of adolescent reading comprehension research (Biancarosa & Snow, 2006; Edmonds et al., 2009; Flynn, Marquis, Paquet, Peeke, & Aubry, 2012; Kamil et al., 2008; Lee & Spratley, 2010) have synthesized practices that are appropriate for all content-area teachers to use. In 2008, the IES published a practice guide after synthesizing our knowledge in regard to these practices (Kamil et al., 2008).

Their intention was to provide a simple set of guidelines to practitioners about how to intervene with adolescents who struggle with reading.

In terms of prevention, three of their recommendations particularly apply. The authors of the guide recommended providing

- direct and explicit vocabulary instruction,
- direct and explicit comprehension strategy instruction, and
- opportunities for extended discussion of text meaning and interpretation.

Some of these practices can be characterized as "teacher-directed" practices aimed at enhancing comprehension. This includes providing background knowledge or instruction in key vocabulary prior to students reading a text.

Students typically come to the secondary level with some background knowledge, but this might not be the right or complete enough knowledge that they need to understand the text they are required to read and learn. Teachers can enhance students' comprehension by providing a short introduction with a video or activity of an overarching, difficult concept that students will encounter in the text they will read. This should take no longer than five to seven minutes. In addition, teachers can preselect a few (e.g., three to five) essential vocabulary words to teach prior to students reading a text (Apthorp et al., 2012).

Teachers can also integrate instruction in strategies that students can use on their own to enhance vocabulary and comprehension—that is, these are strategies students can apply when they do not understand a word or concept. This might include instruction in morphemic analysis, such as how to recognize and use knowledge of prefixes and suffixes to attach meaning to an unknown word (Reed, 2008). Teachers might also explicitly model for students how to get the main idea of a text, which requires them to identify the who/what a section is about and the most important information about that who/what (Vaughn & Klingner, 1999).

Peer-mediated instruction is another promising practice that has evidence of effectiveness at the secondary level (Wexler, Reed, Pyle, Mitchell, & Barton, 2015). Using a systematic peer-mediated reading intervention allows students an opportunity to discuss and interpret text. A multicomponent intervention, collaborative strategic reading (CSR) (Boardman et al., 2016; Vaughn, Klingner, & Bryant, 2001), can be used for prevention purposes in the content-area setting. This set of strategies teaches students how to be strategic readers before, during, and after reading to enhance comprehension of text. It also allows students an opportunity to work collaboratively to discuss and interpret text with peers (Kunsch, Jitendra, & Sood, 2007).

For students with generally lower reading achievement, the use of distinct intervention strategies for comprehension instruction is associated with improved comprehension (Vaughn & Klingner, 2004). These students especially need explicit instruction and practice in how to make sense of text so they are not left to infer meaning on their own. Teachers do not need to provide instruction in a new strategy each day. Adopting a relatively simple instructional practice routine, like CSR, prior to reading should suffice.

Another multicomponent intervention by Vaughn et al. (2013), Promoting Adolescents' Comprehension of Text, or PACT, is an example of an evidence-based instructional routine that teachers can adopt for use across the content areas. PACT consists of providing a comprehension canopy (i.e., background knowledge), essential words instruction (i.e., vocabulary instruction), and critical reading of text (i.e., an opportunity for students to stop and discuss the critical meaning of text). For more information on the PACT intervention, see http://www.meadowscenter.org/projects/detail/promoting-adolescents-comprehension-of-text-pact.

Supplemental Prevention Instruction

If resources are available, schools might consider providing a supplemental class for as many students in need of more preventative instruction as possible. This class typically consists of instruction in a standard protocol intervention, an empirically validated and sometimes scripted program or set of strategies. Group size can range, but the class ideally includes no more than ten to fifteen struggling readers who are slightly below grade level (Vaughn et al., 2010) and is taught by a specialist in place of an elective class for a student.

The instruction that a teacher provides in this class should target skills aimed at enhancing students' ability to read fluently and comprehend text and should align with those strategies taught in the content-area class setting as described above. In addition to the vocabulary and comprehension strategy instruction, a supplemental intervention class is an appropriate setting for instruction in advanced word study. Older students need to be able to decode multisyllabic words fluently in order to comprehend text (Bryant et al., 2000).

Two common ways to teach students to decode multisyllabic words are (1) identifying known parts by using a flexible strategy that identifies known affixes and vowel sounds and (2) decoding the word by using known syllable types (Archer, Gleason, & Vachon, 2003). While both techniques can be used for prevention or remediation (see next section below), typically students in the prevention phase can benefit from learning strategies to help identify known word parts and morphology.

It is also important to provide practice reading connected text to enhance students' ability to read fluently (Stevens, Walker, & Vaughn, 2016). Fluency is necessary for secondary readers to keep up with the large quantities of upper-level text they are required to read. While a great deal remains to be learned regarding fluency development for secondary students, previously documented fluency interventions at the elementary level may be helpful in guiding us in best practices for secondary students. For example, repeated reading techniques and partner reading are two promising evidence-based strategies to build fluency (Fuchs, Fuchs, & Kazdan, 1999).

Instructional steps to implement partner reading are provided in a research brief on fluency instruction found at https://www.texasgateway.org/resource/target-2-research-briefs. It is important to remember, however, that fluency practice alone is not typically sufficient to improve student outcomes in comprehension at the secondary level (Wexler, Vaughn, Roberts, & Denton, 2010). Rather, the correlation between oral reading fluency and comprehension seems to decrease as text becomes more difficult, necessitating that fluency practice be combined with advanced word study and ongoing comprehension strategy instruction to yield higher gains (Paris, Carpenter, Paris, & Hamilton, 2005).

Features of Effective Instruction

Regardless of whether teachers are implementing prevention instruction in the content-area setting or the supplemental class setting, they should not ignore the importance of delivering instruction using features of effective instruction (Archer & Hughes, 2011). As explained in the section about the elementary level above, this means that teachers should use explicit and systematic instruction with modeling, provide many opportunities for students to respond and practice, and give immediate corrective feedback throughout their instruction.

Additionally, progress monitoring is essential to guide decisions regarding instruction once an intervention has been put in place (Torgesen & Miller, 2009; Wayman, Wallace, Wiley, Tichá, & Espin, 2007). These features of effective instruction are useful for all students, but especially critical for meeting the needs of students who struggle academically (Rupley, Blair, & Nichols, 2009).

Planning for Prevention

To plan for prevention, a first step is for school leaders to identify and adopt school-wide literacy strategies that they expect teachers to implement in their content-area classes for all students. Leaders can visit the What Works Clearinghouse (https://ies.ed.gov/ncee/WWC/), a website developed by the U.S. Department of Education IES that reviews the existing research on programs and practices.

School leadership teams should develop fidelity of implementation observation tools to help leaders monitor implementation of key features of the instruction that should not be altered (Reed et al., 2012). The point of monitoring fidelity is not to catch teachers doing something wrong but rather to help interpret whether student progress or lack of progress is due to implementation issues (Swanson, Wanzek, Haring, Ciullo, & McCulley, 2013).

It is also important for school leaders to develop a plan on how they will provide ongoing professional development and support in how to implement this instruction. Administration might also want to consider what other service delivery models are in place and/or how to capitalize on enhanced instruction. For example, some schools may place special education coteachers in their general education content-area classes, in which case they may be able to capitalize on the expertise of that special education instructor (Friend, 2000; Magiera & Zigmond, 2005; Murawski & Swanson, 2001; Scruggs, Mastropieri, & McDuffie, 2007; Solis, Vaughn, Swanson, & McCulley, 2012).

Considering logistics and resources, it is difficult for many schools to administer screening assessments to all students and, in fact, this might not be necessary. The use of a state test as a screener at the secondary level may be a cost-effective, resource-wise tool to identify needy students (Reed et al., 2012). Some students may not have been previously identified as struggling readers, some may just begin to struggle as the content demands of the older grades increase, or some may be new to the district. For all of these students, having general screening measures in place in order to "catch" and identify those who require supplemental support is critical.

REMEDIATION AT THE SECONDARY LEVEL

Another recommendation set forth by the authors of the IES adolescent literacy practice guide (Kamil et al., 2008) is that schools need to make available intensive individualized interventions for struggling readers that can be provided by trained specialists. In other words, we expect that some students in a school will be reading well below grade level, necessitating more intensive intervention to remediate deficits.

By collecting screening information, schools can determine exactly which students these are. Schools may consider using current performance—rather than response to intervention—to identify these students. For example, students performing below the 35th percentile on a state test may be candidates for remediation; therefore, it may be counterproductive and a waste of time and resources to use a model in which students are forced to "prove" that they are very behind by first progressing through a supplemental class aimed at prevention.

Secondary students who are functioning well below their grade level do not have the time to spare and need targeted remediation as soon as possible.

In fact, we know that it is an extremely difficult task to close the gap with typically developing peers once students are in need of remediation (Vaughn, Wexler et al., 2012).

IMPLEMENTING REMEDIAL INTERVENTIONS IN THE SECONDARY GRADES

Remediation of reading difficulties at the secondary level occurs under similar conditions as it does for students in the elementary grades. For secondary students to benefit from remediation efforts in the area of reading difficulties, they will require intensive instruction in some of the same research-based instructional strategies described in this chapter's section on prevention.

The goals of reading and comprehending upper-level text remain the same for these students and—although instruction in the same components of reading are necessary—students in need of remediation will need an instructional emphasis on foundational-level skills as they relate to each reading component. For example, these students likely need more instruction in foundational-level word study than students in need of prevention who may be working on more advanced word study skills (i.e., multisyllabic word reading).

Similar to the elementary grades, the focus of remediation should be on areas where students are struggling as well as explicit strategies for independent reading. Like elementary readers, students at the secondary level will benefit from being able to decode unfamiliar words, develop a vocabulary base to understand meanings of words, use strategies to understand complex text, and read text fluently to succeed as an independent reader.

Older readers must be able to apply this knowledge to a higher level of text and they may have larger gaps to fill before reaching this independent level. Many students profit when they are "armed" with specific tools and strategies to decode and understand words rather than being left to their own coping strategies (Denton, Vaughn, Wexler, Bryan, & Reed, 2012).

Instilling motivation through genuine success is another key ingredient for literary achievement at this level and is one of the recommendations from the IES practice guide (Kamil et al., 2008). On a positive note, while some may doubt the interest and commitment of struggling adolescents to participate in instruction that will improve their skills, researchers have confirmed the fact that even secondary students who have a history of severely struggling with reading recognize the importance of reading proficiency and would likely accept help if provided the opportunity to receive quality instruction (Wexler, Reed, & Sturges, 2015).

Besides providing targeted, effective instruction, teachers can also integrate some deliberate strategies to enhance motivation and ongoing engagement. For example, teachers may explicitly teach students how to set attainable goals and track their own progress. This provides students with greater responsibility for their learning (Stevenson, 2016).

Features of Effective Instruction

As described in the prevention section in this chapter, using features of effective instruction is essential for struggling learners. It is even more essential for students in need of remediation. Teachers can use the features of effective instruction to intensify instruction (Vaughn, Wanzek et al., 2012). Presumably, because remediation classes are ideally smaller than prevention classes, a good teacher will be able to provide even more explicit instruction with many opportunities for students to practice and receive feedback (Hattie & Timperley, 2007).

Planning for Remediation

Planning to put a multitiered system of support in place in a school should encompass planning for prevention and remediation concurrently to account for logistics and resource availability. Through screening, students should be identified who would benefit from remedial efforts. School personnel should carefully consider content needs as well as delivery of instruction when deciding what model will fit the needs of the school(s) and the students. After determining which students are indeed in need of remediation, diagnostic assessments can help interventionists pinpoint the area of need for each student.

Teachers can use a range of informal and formal progress monitoring measures to adapt and individualize intervention (Espin, Wallace, Lembke, Campbell, & Long, 2010; Wayman et al., 2007). Logistically, there are a few features of remediation at the secondary level that school leaders should consider. First, if possible, schools should provide daily intensive reading instruction. This usually occurs during the school day in place of an elective period. Increasing the intensity of instruction by increasing the time in intervention is one way to step up preventative efforts into remedial efforts.

Second, providing an opportunity for increased individualized instruction and feedback by reducing class size can be more effective than trying to remediate a student's gaps in the regular, large-group content classroom. A class for remediation purposes should have five or fewer students (Vaughn et al., 2010). However, teachers should also be aware that a small group size can restrict certain activities (Reed et al., 2012).

The ideal situation in a partner reading pair is to have one person reading at a slightly higher level than his or her partner to provide a model of reading; however, the two students should not be so far apart in ability that they are not capable of providing feedback to each other. In fact, a high school partner reading fluency intervention was compromised because all pairs were composed of homogenous low-level readers (Wexler et al., 2010). Lastly, it is important to provide instruction by a trained teacher who is supported by other school, district, or state personnel, or any outside sources necessary.

CONCLUSION

This chapter has identified elements of a prevention and remediation program for elementary and secondary students with significant reading difficulties or disabilities. Essential to the effective implementation of prevention and remediation programs is a school-wide effort that capitalizes on ongoing screening, diagnostic assessment, instruction, and remediation. Designing a prevention and/or remediation program for elementary and secondary students requires a commitment from the leadership level to the classroom level.

While it is not an easy task, the results are significant and yield a reduced overall need for remediation. When students reach the secondary level, they come with a variety of experiences, background knowledge, and abilities. In order to close the gap and level the playing field for all students, teachers can implement instruction based on research practices so that students do not fall further behind.

POINTS TO REMEMBER

- Use screening measures to identify students who are at risk. Some of this information may be attainable through existing data (e.g., state tests).
- Monitor progress regularly to pinpoint and continuously adapt instruction and intervention for students receiving supplemental prevention and remediation support.
- Integrate evidence-based reading instruction into the general education setting at the elementary level and content-area classes at the secondary level to provide prevention support to all students.
- Struggling readers may need supplemental prevention and/or remediation support. Students in need of remediation will need a focus on foundational-level skills in smaller groups and for more time during intervention.
- Use features of effective instruction (e.g., explicit instruction and modeling, immediate corrective feedback) when delivering instruction in all settings and use these features to intensify support for students in supplemental prevention and remediation settings.

REFERENCES

ACT Inc. (2009). *Measuring college and career readiness: The class of 2009*. Retrieved from http://files.eric.ed.gov/fulltext/ED506463.pdf

ACT Inc. (2013). *The condition of college & career readiness*. Retrieved from http://files.eric.ed.gov/fulltext/ED546777.pdf

Apthorp, H., Randel, B., Cherasaro, T., Clark, T., McKeown, M., & Beck, I. (2012). Effects of a supplemental vocabulary program on word knowledge and passage comprehension. *Journal of Research on Educational Effectiveness, 5*, 160–188.

Archer, A. L., Gleason, M. M., & Vachon, V. L. (2003). Decoding and fluency: Foundation skills for struggling older readers. *Learning Disability Quarterly, 26*, 89–101.

Archer, A. L., & Hughes, C. A. (2011). Exploring the foundations of explicit instruction. In K. R. Harris & S. Graham (Eds.), *Explicit instruction: Effective and efficient teaching* (pp. 1–22). New York, NY: Guilford Press.

Beck, I. L., & McKeown, M. G. (2007). Increasing young low-income children's oral vocabulary repertoires through rich and focused instruction. *Elementary School Journal, 107*, 251–271.

Beck, I. L., McKeown, M. G., & Kucan, L. (2002). *Bringing words to life*. New York, NY: Guilford Press.

Biancarosa, G., & Snow, C. E. (2006). *Reading next—a vision for action and research in middle and high school literacy: A report to the Carnegie Corporation of New York*. Washington, DC: Alliance for Excellent Education.

Blachman, B. A. (2000). Phonological awareness. In M. L. Kamil, P. B. Mosenthal, P. D. Pearson, & R. Barr (Eds.), *Handbook of reading research* (pp. 483–502). Mahwah, NJ: Lawrence Erlbaum.

Boardman, A. G., Buckley, P., Vaughn, S., Roberts, G., Scomavacco, K., & Klingner, J. K. (2016). Relationship between implementation of collaborative strategic reading and student outcomes for adolescents with disabilities. *Journal of Learning Disabilities, 49*(6), 644–657.

Bowers, P. N., Kirby, J. R., & Deacon, S. H. (2010). The effects of morphological instruction on literacy skills: A systematic review of the literature. *Review of Educational Research, 80*, 144–179.

Bryant, D. P., Vaughn, S., Linan-Thompson, S., Ugel, N., Hamff, A., & Hougen, M. (2000). Reading outcomes for students with and without reading disabilities in general education middle-school content area classes. *Learning Disability Quarterly, 23*, 238–252.

Carlisle, J. F. (2010). Effects of instruction in morphological awareness on literacy achievement: An integrative review. *Reading Research Quarterly, 45*, 464–487.

Carney, K. J., & Stiefel, G. S. (2008). Long-term results of a problem-solving approach to response to intervention: Discussion and implications. *Learning Disabilities: A Contemporary Journal, 6*(2), 61–75.

Connor, C. M., Alberto, P. A., Compton, D. L., & O'Connor, R. E. (2014). *Improving reading outcomes for students with or at risk for reading disabilities: A synthesis of the contributions from the Institute of Education Sciences Research Centers* (NCSER 20143000). Washington, DC: National Center for Special Education Research, Institute of Education Sciences, U.S. Department of Education.

Denton, C. A., Vaughn, S., Wexler, J., Bryan, D., & Reed, D. (2012). *Effective instruction for middle school students with reading difficulties: The reading teacher's sourcebook*. Baltimore, MD: Brookes.

Edmonds, M. S., Vaughn, S., Wexler, J., Reutebuch, C., Cable, A., Tackett, K. K., & Schnakenberg, J. W. (2009). A synthesis of reading interventions and effects on reading comprehension outcomes for older struggling readers. *Review of Educational Research, 79*(1), 262–300.

Elleman, A. M., Lindo, E. J., Morphy, P., & Compton, D. L. (2009). The impact of vocabulary instruction on passage-level comprehension of school-age children: A meta-analysis. *Journal of Research on Educational Effectiveness, 2*, 1–44.

Espin, C., Wallace, T., Lembke, E., Campbell, H., & Long, J. D. (2010). Creating a progress monitoring system in reading for middle-school students: Tracking progress toward meeting high-stakes standards. *Learning Disabilities Research & Practice, 25*(2), 60–75.

Flynn, R. J., Marquis, R. A., Paquet, M. P., Peeke, L. M., & Aubry, T. D. (2012). Effects of individual direct-instruction tutoring on foster children's academic skills: A randomized trial. *Children and Youth Services Review, 34*(6), 1183–1189.

Foorman, B., & Wanzek, J. (2016). Classroom reading instruction for all students. In S. R. Jimerson, M. K. Burns, & A. M. VanDerHeyden (Eds.), *Handbook of response to intervention: The science and practice of multi-tiered systems of support* (2nd ed.) (pp. 232–252). New York, NY: Springer.

Friend, M. (2000). *Interactions: Collaboration skills for school professionals*. New York, NY: Longman.

Fuchs, D., Compton, D. L., Fuchs, L. S., Bryant, V. J., Hamlett, C. L., & Lambert, W. (2012). First-grade cognitive abilities as long-term predictors of reading comprehension and disability status. *Journal of Learning Disabilities, 45*, 217–231.

Fuchs, L. S., & Fuchs, D. (2011). *Using CBM for progress monitoring in reading*. Washington, DC: National Center on Student Progress Monitoring.

Fuchs, L. S., Fuchs, D., & Kazdan, S. (1999). Effects of peer-assisted learning strategies on high school students with serious reading problems. *Remedial and Special Education, 20*, 309–319.

Gersten, R., Fuchs, L. S., Williams, J. P., & Baker, S. (2001). Teaching reading comprehension strategies to students with learning disabilities: A review of research. *Review of Educational Research, 71*(2), 279–320.

Hattie, J., & Timperley, H. (2007). The power of feedback. *Review of Educational Research, 77*, 81–112.

Heller, R., & Greenleaf, C. L. (2007). *Literacy instruction in the content areas: Getting to the core of middle and high school improvement* (Report). Washington, DC: Alliance for Excellent Education.

Hernandez, D. J. (2012). *Double jeopardy: How third grade reading skills and poverty influence high school graduation*. Retrieved from http://www.aecf.org/KnowledgeCenter/Publications.aspx?pubguid={8E2B6F93-75C6-4AA6-8C6E-CE88945980A9}

Institute of Education Sciences, National Center for Special Education Research. (2006, July). *Facts from NLTS2: General education participation and academic performance of students with learning disabilities* (NCSER 2006-3001). Retrieved from https://ies.ed.gov/ncser/pubs/20063001/index.asp

Kamil, M. L., Borman, G. D., Dole, J., Kral, C. C., Salinger, T., & Torgesen, J. (2008). *Improving adolescent literacy: Effective classroom and intervention practices. A practice guide* (NCEE #2008-4027). Washington, DC: National Center for Education Evaluation and Regional Assistance, Institute of Education Sciences, U.S. Department of Education. Retrieved from http://ies.ed.gov/ncee/wwc

Kershaw, S., & Schatschneider, C. (2012). A latent variable approach to the simple view of reading. *Reading and Writing, 25*(2), 433–464.

Kim, Y.-S., Wagner, R. K., & Lopez, D. (2012). Developmental relations between reading fluency and reading comprehension: A longitudinal study from grade 1 to grade 2. *Journal of Experimental Child Psychology, 113*, 93–111.

Kunsch, C. A., Jitendra, A. K., & Sood, S. (2007). The effects of peer-mediated instruction in mathematics for students with learning problems: A research synthesis. *Learning Disabilities Research & Practice, 22*(1), 1–12.

Lai, S. A., Benjamin, R. G., Schwanenflugel, P. J., & Kuhn, M. R. (2014). The longitudinal relationship between reading fluency and reading comprehension skills in second-grade children. *Reading and Writing Quarterly, 30*, 116–138.

Lee, C. D., & Spratley, A. (2010). *Reading in the disciplines: The challenges of adolescent literacy* (Final Report from Carnegie Corporation of New York's Council on Advancing Adolescent Literacy). New York, NY: Carnegie Corporation of New York.

Liberman, I. Y., & Shankweiler, D. (2013). Phonology and beginning reading: A tutorial. In L. Rieben & C. A. Perfetti (Eds.), *Learning to read: Basic research and its implication* (pp. 3–18). New York, NY: Routledge.

Luftus, S. M., Coyne, M. D., McCoach, D. B., Zipoli, R., & Pullen, P. C. (2010). Effects of a supplemental vocabulary intervention on the word knowledge of kindergarten students at risk for language and literacy difficulties. *Learning Disabilities Research & Practice, 25,* 124–136.

Magiera, K., & Zigmond, N. (2005). Co-teaching in middle school classrooms under routine conditions: Does the instructional experience differ for students with disabilities in cotaught and solo-taught classes? *Learning Disabilities Research & Practice, 20*(2), 79–85.

McKeown, M. G., Beck, I. L., & Blake, R. G. K. (2009). Rethinking reading comprehension instruction: A comparison of instruction for strategies and content approaches. *Research Quarterly, 44,* 218–253.

McLaughlin, M. (2012). Reading comprehension: What every teacher needs to know. *The Reading Teacher, 65,* 432–440.

Morgan, P. L., Sideridis, G., & Hua, Y. (2012). Initial and over-time effects of fluency interventions for students with or at risk for disabilities. *Journal of Special Education, 46,* 94–116.

Murawski, W. W., & Swanson, H. L. (2001). Meta-analysis of co-teaching research: Where are the data? *Remedial and Special Education, 22*(5), 258–267.

National Center for Education Statistics. (2015a). *The nation's report card. 2015: Mathematics & reading assessments.* Washington, DC: U.S. Department of Education. Retrieved from http://www.nationsreportcard.gov/reading_math_2015/#?grade=8

National Center for Education Statistics. (2015b). *The nation's report card. 2015: Mathematics & reading at grade 12.* Washington, DC: U.S. Department of Education. Retrieved from http://www.nationsreportcard.gov/reading_math_g12_2015/#reading

National Early Literacy Panel. (2009). *Developing early literacy: Report of the National Early Literacy Panel.* Washington, DC: National Institute for Literacy.

National Governors Association Center for Best Practices & Council of Chief State School Officers. (2010). *Common Core State Standards: Application to students with disabilities.* Washington, DC. Retrieved from http://www.corestandards.org/

National Reading Panel. (2000). *Teaching children to read: An evidence-based assessment of the scientific research literature on reading and its implications for reading instruction.* Washington, DC: U.S. Government Printing Office.

Next Generation Science Standards Lead States. (2013). *Next Generation Science Standards: For states, by states.* Washington, DC: National Academies Press.

Nunes, T., Bryant, P., & Barros, R. (2012). The development of word recognition and its significance for comprehension and fluency. *Journal of Educational Psychology, 104,* 959–973.

O'Connor, R. (2014). *Teaching word recognition: Effective strategies for students with learning difficulties.* New York, NY: Guilford Press.

O'Connor, R. E., Bocian, K. M., Beach, K. D., Sanchez, V., & Flynn, L. J. (2013). Special education in a 4-year response to intervention (RtI) environment: Characteristics of students with learning disability and grade of identification. *Learning Disabilities Research & Practice, 28,* 98–112.

O'Shaughnessy, T. E., & Swanson, H. L. (2000). A comparison of two reading interventions for children with reading disabilities. *Journal of Learning Disabilities, 33,* 257–277.

Paris, S. G., Carpenter, R. D., Paris, A. H., & Hamilton, E. E. (2005). Spurious and genuine correlates of children's reading comprehension. In S. G. Paris & S. A. Stahl (Eds.), *Children's reading comprehension and assessment* (pp. 131–160). Mahwah, NJ: Erlbaum.

Reed, D. K. (2008). A synthesis of morphology interventions and effects on reading outcomes for students in grades K–12. *Learning Disabilities Research & Practice, 23*(1), 36–49.

Reed, D. K., Wexler, J., & Vaughn, S. (2012). *RTI for reading at the secondary level: Recommended literacy practices and remaining questions.* New York, NY: Guilford Press.

Rupley, W. H., Blair, T. R., & Nichols, W. D. (2009). Effective reading instruction for struggling readers: The role of direct/explicit teaching. *Reading & Writing Quarterly, 25*(2), 125–138.

Sáenz, L. M., & Fuchs, L. S. (2002). Examining the reading difficulty of secondary students with learning disabilities expository versus narrative text. *Remedial and Special Education, 23*(1), 31–41.

Scruggs, T. E., Mastropieri, M. A., & McDuffie, K. A. (2007). Co-teaching in inclusive classrooms: A metasynthesis of qualitative research. *Exceptional Children, 73*(4), 392–416.

Shanahan, T., & Shanahan, C. (2008). Teaching disciplinary literacy to adolescents: Rethinking content-area literacy. *Harvard Educational Review, 78*, 40–59.

Shany, M., & Biemiller, A. (2010). Individual differences in reading comprehension gains assisted reading practice: Preexisting conditions, vocabulary acquisition, and amounts of practice. *Reading and Writing, 23*, 1071–1083.

Silverman, R. D., Speece, D. L., Harring, J. R., & Ritchey, K. D. (2013). Fluency has a role in the simple view of reading. *Scientific Studies of Reading, 17*, 108–133.

Solis, M., Vaughn, S., Swanson, E., & McCulley, L. (2012). Collaborative models of instruction: The empirical foundations of inclusion and co-teaching. *Psychology in the Schools, 49*(5), 498–511.

Stahl, S. A., & Fairbanks, M. M. (2006). The effects of vocabulary instruction. In K. A. Dougherty-Stahl & M. C. McKenna (Eds.), *Reading research at work* (pp. 226–261). New York, NY: Guilford.

Stanovich, K. E. (1986). Matthew effects in reading: Some consequences of individual differences in the acquisition of literacy. *Reading Research Quarterly, 21*, 360–407.

Stevens, E. A., Walker, M. A., & Vaughn, S. (2016). The effects of reading fluency interventions on the reading fluency and reading comprehension performance of elementary students with learning disabilities: A synthesis of the research from 2001 to 2014. *Journal of Learning Disabilities, 50*(5), 576–590. doi:10.1177/0022219416638028

Stevenson, N. (2016). Effects of planning and goal setting on reducing latency to task engagement for struggling readers in middle school. *Journal of Behavioral Education, 25*(2), 206–222.

Suggate, S. P. (2016). A meta-analysis of the long-term effects of phonemic awareness, phonics, fluency, and reading comprehension interventions. *Journal of Learning Disabilities, 49*, 77–96.

Swanson, E., Wanzek, J., Haring, C., Ciullo, S., & McCulley, L. (2013). Intervention fidelity in special and general education research journals. *Journal of Special Education, 47*(1), 3–13.

Swanson, E., Wanzek, J., McCulley, L., Stillman, S., Vaughn, S., Simmons, D., … Hairrell, A. (2015). Literacy and text reading in middle and high school social studies and English language arts classrooms. *Reading and Writing Quarterly 32*(3), 199–222. doi:10573569.2014.910718

Torgesen, J. K., Alexander, A. W., Wagner, R. K., Rashotte, C. A., Voeller, K. K. S., & Conway, T. (2001). Intensive remedial instruction for children with severe reading disabilities: Immediate and long-term outcomes from two instructional approaches. *Journal of Learning Disabilities, 34*, 33–58.

Torgesen, J. K., & Miller, D. H. (2009). *Assessments to guide adolescent literacy instruction.* Portsmouth, NH: RMC Research Corporation, Center on Instruction.

Tuckwiller, E. D., Pullen, P. C., & Coyne, M. D. (2010). The use of the regression discontinuity design in tiered intervention research: A pilot study exploring vocabulary instruction for at-risk kindergarteners. *Learning Disabilities Research & Practice, 25*, 137–150.

Vaughn, S., & Klingner, J. K. (1999). Teaching reading comprehension through collaborative strategic reading. *Intervention in School and Clinic, 34*(5), 284–292.

Vaughn, S., & Klingner, J. K. (2004). Teaching reading comprehension to students with learning disabilities. In C. A. Stone, E. R. Silliman, B. J. Ehren, & K. Apel (Eds.), *Challenges in language and literacy: Handbook of language and literacy; Development and disorders* (pp. 541–555). New York, NY: Guilford Press.

Vaughn, S., Klingner, J. K., & Bryant, D. P. (2001). Collaborative strategic reading as a means to enhance peer-mediated instruction for reading comprehension and content-area learning. *Remedial and Special Education, 22*(2), 66–74.

Vaughn, S., Swanson, E. A., Roberts, G., Wanzek, J., Stillman-Spisak, S. J., Solis, M., & Simmons, D. (2013). Improving reading comprehension and social studies knowledge in middle school. *Reading Research Quarterly, 48*(1), 77–93.

Vaughn, S., Wanzek, J., Murray, C. S., & Roberts, G. (2012). *Intensive interventions for students struggling in reading and mathematics: A practice guide.* Portsmouth, NH: RMC Research, Center on Instruction.

Vaughn, S., Wanzek, J., Wexler, J., Barth, A., Cirino, P. T., Fletcher, J. M., . . . Francis, D. (2010). The relative effects of group size on reading progress of older students with reading difficulties. *Reading and Writing: An Interdisciplinary Journal, 23*, 931–956.

Vaughn, S., Wexler, J., Leroux, A., Roberts, G., Denton, C. A., Barth, A., & Fletcher, J. (2012). Effects of an intensive reading intervention for eighth grade students with persistently inadequate response to intervention. *Journal of Learning Disabilities, 45*(6), 515–525.

Vellutino, F. R., Scanlon, D. M., & Jaccard, J. (2003). Toward distinguishing between cognitive and experiential deficits as primary sources of difficulty in learning to read: A two year follow-up of difficult to remediate and readily remediated poor readers. In B. R. Foorman (Ed.), *Preventing and remediating reading difficulties: Bringing science to scale* (pp. 73–120). Baltimore, MD: York Press.

Wanzek, J., & Vaughn, S. (2011). Is a three-tier reading intervention model associated with reduced placement in special education? *Remedial and Special Education, 32*, 167–175.

Wanzek, J., Vaughn, S., Scammacca, N., Gatlin, B., Walker, M. A., & Capin, P. (2016). Meta-analyses of the effects of tier 2 type reading interventions in grades K–3. *Educational Psychology Review, 28*, 551–576.

Wanzek, J., Wexler, J., Vaughn, S., & Ciullo, S. (2010). Reading interventions for struggling readers in the upper elementary grades: A synthesis of 20 years of research. *Reading and Writing: An Interdisciplinary Journal, 23*, 889–912.

Wayman, M. M., Wallace, T., Wiley, H. I., Tichá, R., & Espin, C. A. (2007). Literature synthesis on curriculum-based measurement in reading. *Journal of Special Education, 41*(2), 85–120.

Wexler, J., Mitchell, M. A., Clancy, E. E., & Silverman, R. D. (2016). An investigation of literacy practices in high school science classrooms. *Reading & Writing Quarterly, 33*(3), 258–277. doi:10.1080/10573569.2016.1193832

Wexler, J., Reed, D. K., Pyle, N., Mitchell, M., & Barton, E. E. (2015). A synthesis of peer mediated academic interventions for secondary struggling learners. *Journal of Learning Disabilities, 48*(5), 451–470.

Wexler, J., Reed, D. K., & Sturges, K. M. (2015). Reading practices in the juvenile correctional facility setting: Incarcerated adolescents speak out. *Exceptionality, 23*(2), 100–123.

Wexler, J., Vaughn, S., Roberts, G., & Denton, C. A. (2010). The efficacy of repeated reading and wide reading practice for high school students with severe reading disabilities. *Learning Disabilities: Research & Practice, 25*, 2–10.

Chapter Three

Understanding and Promoting the Motivation to Read in Young Children

Elizabeth Jean, Paul L. Morgan, and Doug Fuchs

Motivation to read has been defined by Gambrell (2011) as "the likelihood of engaging in reading or choosing to read" (p. 172) and is the "key to developing successful readers" (Strategic Marketing & Research Inc., 2013, p. 8). Both researchers and practitioners alike view it as critically important that children become and remain motivated to read frequently (Gambrell & Marinak, 2010; Strategic Marketing & Research Inc., 2013; Ahmadi, 2017).

Seminal work completed by Guthrie and Wigfield (1999, 2000) identified motivation as the "preeminent predictor" (Guthrie & Wigfield, 1999, p. 250) of frequent reading; they further state that "motivation is what activates [reading] behavior" (Guthrie & Wigfield, 2000, p. 405). In turn, frequent reading practice contributes to growth in the skills necessary to become a proficient, lifelong reader. These skills include sight word recognition, vocabulary, verbal fluency, reading comprehension, and general knowledge (Gambrell & Marinak, 2010, Ciampa, 2012; Strategic Marketing & Research Inc., 2013).

Unfortunately, those most likely to benefit from frequent reading practice, the poor readers, are often unmotivated to do so (Melekoglu & Wilkerson, 2013; Strategic Marketing & Research Inc., 2013). This lack of motivation begins to appear within a few years of school entry (Castle, 2015; Torres, 2010; Froiland, Oros, Smith, & Hirchert, 2012). Because of its link to reading practice, poor readers' lack of motivation is strongly suggested as a primary cause of long-term reading difficulties (Ciampa, 2012; Cambria & Guthrie, 2010; Torres, 2010; Strategic Marketing & Research Inc., 2013).

One frequently studied explanation as to why poor readers are unmotivated to practice reading is that children become poorly motivated because

41

they repeatedly fail at acquiring reading skills (Strategic Marketing & Research Inc., 2013; Morgan, 2013; Stanovich, 1986). For example, Stanovich (1986) hypothesized, and Morgan (2013) agreed, that reading difficulties cause "behavioral/ cognitive/motivational spinoffs" (Stanovich, 1986, p. 389), or "negative Matthew effects" (Stanovich, 1986, p. 360).

The Matthew effect, based on the Bible verse Matthew 25:29, suggests that the poor get poorer while the rich get richer. In terms of reading motivation and skill acquisition, the more an individual reads the more confident that person becomes, while conversely, the less an individual reads the more difficulty he or she encounters. Stanovich (1986) took it one step further, stating that there is a widening gap between slow and fast starters due to the Matthew effect, a concept that has been explored in other studies as well (Ahmadi, 2017; Melekoglu & Wilkerson, 2013).

MIXED EVIDENCE ON THE RELATION BETWEEN POOR READING PERFORMANCE AND MOTIVATION

While most young children enter school with an innate excitement to read, it is necessary to understand if reading difficulties lead students to become poorly motivated to practice reading. Surprisingly, the evidence is somewhat mixed.

In some studies, children's reading skills and reading motivation correlate moderately (Ciampa, 2012; Morgan, 2013; Edmunds & Bauserman, 2006). To prove this point, Ciampa (2012) states, "Motivation to read is both the essential element for actively engaging young children in the reading process and a strong predictor of later reading skills" (p. 2). Studies by Hall (2014), Carroll and Fox (2017), and Hornery, Seaton, Tracey, Craven, and Yeung (2014) contradicted these results and found reading skills and reading self-concepts correlated only weakly.

McGeown, Norgate, and Warhurst (2012) found that neither standardized reading scores nor teacher ratings of seven- and eight-year-old children's reading ability significantly predicted their intrinsic reading motivation at age nine. Instead, early reading motivation predicted later reading ability and "conversely, students who struggle begin to doubt their ability" (Cambria & Guthrie, 2010, p. 17; Guthrie, Wigfield, & You, 2012; Schaffner, Schiefele, & Ulferts, 2013). Finally, in face-to-face interviews with students, Edmunds and Bauserman (2006) discovered that "student level of motivation varied as much as the students themselves" (p. 414), a point that Gambrell (2011) and Cambria and Guthrie (2010) agreed with.

METHODOLOGICAL REASONS FOR THESE MIXED FINDINGS

Methodological reasons help to explain these mixed findings. Most studies to date have relied on samples of young children displaying a full range of reading abilities and a plethora of dimensions of reading that relate directly to reading motivation (Schiefele, Schaffner, Moller, & Wigfield, 2012; McGeown et al., 2012). Use of these full-range samples may act to hide the effect's initial emergence because most young children experience a range of success and difficulty in learning to read; thus, it may be several years before the children's performance in reading stabilizes and begins influencing their reading motivation (Schiefele et al., 2012; McGeown et al., 2012).

In contrast, some children with phonological deficits may experience relatively consistent failure learning to read, and it is these same children who are likely to display early declines in motivation and become weaker readers over time (Snowling & Hulme, 2013; Ciampa, 2012). Few investigators have used quasi- or true-experimental designs in which they manipulate the hypothesized causal agent, that of progress in acquiring reading skills.

Researchers have relied, instead, on descriptive studies (Morgan, 2013; Castle, 2015; Melekoglu & Wilkerson, 2013). Yet causal inferences based only on descriptive studies are circumspect, especially if plausible confounds such as a child's earlier level of motivation and socioeconomic status have not been controlled (Melekoglu & Wilkerson, 2013; Castle, 2015). For these reasons, the reading skills–reading motivation relation remains limited.

Questions persist whether poor readers' low levels of motivation are due to initial difficulties acquiring reading skills or if that these children enter school already more likely to view reading negatively. That is, do poor readers begin their school careers lagging behind their peers in both "skill" and "will"? The answer to this question is important. If young children are poorly motivated because of repeated failure in acquiring reading skills, then this would suggest that educators and staff should focus primarily on remediating their skill deficits. Doing so should lead to gains in their motivation and, eventually, their frequency of reading practice.

Conversely, if poor motivation arises from altogether different factors, for example, a lack of initiative on the part of the family, then this would suggest that practitioners should use interventions that effectively target both skill- and motivation-specific deficits. Families are uniquely poised to increase reading motivation in young readers and as such must understand the role they play. Both families of young children and educators have a responsibility to teach both skill and will, which can be accomplished with a variety of techniques, strategies, and practices.

HOW TO INFLUENCE SKILL AND WILL IN YOUNG CHILDREN

Families and educators play significant roles in influencing skill and will in young readers. It is both skill and will that produce students who are confident readers. Skilled readers know how to "interact with a text, thinking about what will happen next, creating questions" (Strategic Marketing & Research Inc., 2013, p. 7). A number of pundits offer suggestions on the appropriate action items needed to produce lifelong readers (Frey, 2015; U.S. Department of Education, 2016; Fox, 2014; Gambrell, 2011; Ciampa, 2012; Cambria & Guthrie, 2010). What follows is a collection of suggestions for both families and educators to promote reading skill and motivation.

THE ROLE OF FAMILY IN PROMOTING SKILL AND MOTIVATION

Family is a child's first exposure to reading and, thus, plays a pivotal role in early literacy. As such, it is incumbent on families to ensure children have a multitude of varied experiences with all parts of reading to increase motivation; this includes all types of print exposure from a very young age. According to a report published by Strategic Marketing & Research Inc. (2013), "The more a child is exposed to reading, the more likely the child is to acquire the requisite skills for reading" (p. 6).

Evidence suggests that in families where reading is not a priority, motivation is low (Frey, 2015; Cambria & Guthrie, 2010). These homes tend to have fewer books, less time where young children are read to, or even spoken to, and fewer experiences in the world around them. It is this group that begins school with fewer internal resources, word choice, and less motivation. Conversely, children who spent their first years in a print/language-rich environment tend to begin school with a greater sense of motivation and confidence in reading (Frey, 2015, Cambria & Guthrie, 2010).

Print/language-rich homes read daily, have consistent and varied conversation, and have experiences outside of the home on a regular basis. The National Center for Education Statistics (NCES) surveyed families in 2001 and again in 2012 and found that home literacy experiences that emphasized skill and will were higher in 2012 (U.S. Department of Education, 2016). Several authors (Frey, 2015; U.S. Department of Education, 2016; Fox, 2014) suggest the following list of action steps meant to increase motivation on the home front:

- Reading aloud: Perhaps the most common of the list, reading aloud connects the reader, the listener, and the book, creating a dynamic connection, building knowledge, understanding, and a love of reading (Frey, 2015).

Families where reading is a daily activity tend to have children with a higher will to read once they enter school. According to the National Center for Education Statistics (U.S. Department of Education, 2016), in 2012, 83 percent of children who were not yet enrolled in preschool or kindergarten were read to at least three times in one week (U.S. Department of Education, 2016).

- Practicing letters, numbers, and words: According to the NCES report (U.S. Department of Education, 2016), in the week prior to the survey, 98 percent of families who had children aged three to five who were not enrolled in preschool or kindergarten stated they taught their preschoolers numbers, letters, or words. This valuable skill builder had increased from 2001 when only 94 percent of the families responded that they had taught those skills.

- Interaction with books: Daily interactions with books are important for young children. Just as important is that children see the adults around them interacting with print of all kinds, such as newspapers, magazines, food labels. A print-rich home increases a child's ability to feel comfortable with print, understand it, master it, thus creating a space for proficiency that in turn promotes motivation.

- Library and bookstore visits: Families who visit libraries and bookstores instill the importance of books and reading to their children. Often, libraries have story hours for young children. The National Center for Education Statistics (U.S. Department of Education, 2016) found that in 2012 at least 42 percent of families visited a library in the month prior to the study. In Springfield, Massachusetts, the public library website touts story time at several city library branches on different days and at different times, with such offerings as a family story time, bilingual story time, music, crafts, a teddy bear picnic, and a lunch bunch (Springfield Public Library, 2017). These activities show young children not only the importance of reading but that it can be fun and done anywhere, at any time.

- Quiet reading: The opposite of read-alouds, quiet reading gives children time to experience books on their own. Creating a quiet space just for reading can be an added bonus and gives young readers a sense of independence. Coming back together to discuss what has been read is one way to ensure the reader is comprehending the book.

- Sharing a love of books: A family who shares books creates a sense of comfort with reading that translates into a stronger will to read in young children. Hard copy books are inviting and can be held; however, some digital natives may find e-books more engaging (Fox, 2014).

- Car games: Games are always a fun way to become comfortable with reading. In the car, an easy game to play is License to Ride. Much like hide-and-seek, children have to find specific letters and numbers on license plates. Older children may enjoy creating sentences based on license plates, the sillier the better. Finding a word that starts with a particular letter or finding a set of themed words are also great skill builders (Provencher, 2014).

THE ROLE OF EDUCATOR IN PROMOTING SKILL AND MOTIVATION

The role of the educator in developing a strong sense of skill and will cannot be overlooked. Reading skills are usually taught within the school curriculum and include "phonemic awareness, phonics word recognition, vocabulary and simple comprehension" (Cambria & Guthrie, 2010). While it is more difficult to develop a sense of motivation once in school, it is not impossible. Students need both skill and will to be successful lifelong readers.

Cambria and Guthrie (2010) argue that the will, or motivation, is more important of the two. Several authors (Gambrell, 2011; Ciampa, 2012; Fox, 2014; Cambria & Guthrie, 2010) suggest that will exists when certain motivational factors are present in the classroom. Additionally, skill deficits must be addressed by educators to improve motivation. Below is a list of nine factors; each includes a tip on how an educator might update his or her practice to motivate students.

Relevant Reading Tasks

Students who make connections between their lives and what they read are more connected and engaged. They tend to comprehend the text better due to previous scaffolding. According to Hulleman, Godes, Hendricks, and Harackiewicz (2010), students who wrote about something familiar were more motivated. In order to have students become more aware of the relevance of reading tasks, educators should have students keep a journal where they keep track of what they read. Educators should also encourage students to reflect and write for a few minutes to connect what they read to their personal life.

Access to a Variety of Reading Materials

Classrooms replete with books communicate that reading is important and worthwhile. It is also important for an educator to have "an array of genres and text types, magazines, and real-life documents" (Gambrell, 2011, p. 173). A tip to increase student access to reading includes read-alouds and "book-selling sessions" (Gambrell, 2011, p. 174) in which the educator gives a quick book share so that students become aware of the many books in the classroom library and may then be more apt to select those books.

Engagement in Sustained Reading

Sustained reading promotes "motivated and proficient readers" (Gambrell, 2011, p. 174).

A 2006 study by Foorman, Schatschneider, Eakin, Fletcher, Moats, and Francis (as cited in Gambrell, 2011), looked at first- and second-grade students and found that "the amount of time allocated to text reading was positively associated with growth in reading proficiency" (p. 174). The summer slide is often associated with a lack of reading. Educators who want to improve student reading and motivation can encourage students to read over the summer and keep a log of how long and what was read. Turning the log in on the first day of school for an extrinsic prize is an added benefit.

Choosing What to Read and How to Complete Literacy Tasks

Studies indicate that when students have choice over what they read as well as when and how they learn, they are more motivated and understand the material better (Jang, Reeve, & Deci, 2010). To ensure student choice at the appropriate reading level, thus eliminating reading frustration, educators can try "bounded choice" (Gambrell, 2011, p. 175). Here the educator chooses several books within the student reading range and interest level and the student may choose from that group of books.

Social Interaction regarding Texts

Communicating with others is an important part of being motivated to read. Discussion may happen verbally or in written form and includes talking about books, reading in tandem or groups, peer discussions, and the borrowing and sharing of books (Alber, 2014). As a way to increase social interactions surrounding texts, educators may choose to have students read a text then do a "pair/share" or "turn and talk" where they share the information with a partner and then share out with the larger group.

Success with Challenging Texts

When students come across a challenging text, they may be apt to give up. Educators are tasked, then, with finding moderately challenging texts and tasks that students can accomplish, "resulting in increased feelings of competence and increased motivation" (Gambrell, 2011, p. 176). It is suggested that the educator labels classroom bookshelves as hard/harder/hardest, instead of easy/average/difficult. This will engage struggling readers in a book that is more their level whereas a book marked as "easy" may not challenge the student at all.

The Value of Reading Is Reflected in Classroom Incentives

Students are more motivated to read when they feel the educator is providing "constructive and supportive . . . feedback" (Gambrell, 2011, p. 177). Additionally, "specific, elaborated, and embellished teacher praise" was more powerful than extrinsic rewards (Gambrell, 2011, p. 177). Praise, when interpreted as an acknowledgment of achievement, can increase student motivation. However, using extrinsic rewards do work under certain circumstances. A tip to use here is to use books as a reward. For example, if a student reads twenty-five books, the student may choose a new book to keep, or if the books in the classroom library belong to the teacher, the teacher may offer a day when students may choose a book to take home and keep. This shows the importance of books in several ways.

Combining Technology and Reading

In a recent study (Fox, 2014) that integrated technology and reading, it was found that children who used both e-books with audio support and traditional books developed a stronger will to read than those who read exclusively from traditional paper books. Their motivation and self-esteem rose dramatically (Fox, 2014). In order to make a successful transition from the traditional book only to the e-book/traditional book combination, it is important for students to first listen to the e-book, then listen and follow along in the traditional book. Multiple readings are always encouraged and foster a greater sense of competence.

Attacking Skill and Will Deficits Simultaneously

Educators have traditionally used word-level identification strategies to improve children's reading motivation (Denton & Otaiba, 2011; Snowling & Hulme, 2013). A better strategy may be to combine word-level strategies instruction with techniques that specifically target lagging motivation. In short, targeting a poor reader's skill may be a necessary but insufficient approach when increasing his or her motivation is the goal. It may also be necessary to target his or her "will" (Ahmadi, 2017; Castle, 2015).

CONCLUSION

The findings presented at the beginning of the chapter suggest that poor readers' lack of motivation and task engagement may begin to lag very early in their development, perhaps even before school entry; thus, poor readers may enter kindergarten or first-grade classrooms already doubly disadvantaged, in that they begin school possessing both low reading skills and less interest in reading than their peers. This is because struggling readers do not always lack the motivation to read, but often "do not experience progress and competence" when reading (Becker, McElvary, & Kortenbruck, 2010).

Families should use the strategies listed to engage young readers, promoting reading skill and will so that they enter school prepared and willing to learn. Additionally, practitioners may need to be prepared to focus early intervention efforts on deficits in both skill and will if they are to best help students grow to become lifelong readers. Several authors (Edmunds & Bauserman, 2006; Gambrell, 2011; Cambria & Guthrie, 2010; Fox, 2014) detail a variety of techniques that families and practitioners can build into their existing curricula to help bolster struggling readers' motivation.

POINTS TO REMEMBER

- Reading behaviors are activated by motivation. Frequent reading promotes basic reading skills such as sight word recognition, increased vocabulary, fluency, and comprehension.
- The Matthew effect says that good readers read more and poor readers read less, which widens the gap between proficient and struggling readers.
- Skill and will are the preeminent factors that most influence early reading proficiency.
- Families should focus on a print-rich environment at home, incorporating read-alouds and trips to the library as ways to improve will and skill in young readers.
- Practitioners should focus on early intervention strategies that include combining word-level strategy instruction with motivational techniques to increase reading success over a student's lifetime.

REFERENCES

Ahmadi, M. R. (2017). The impact of motivation on reading comprehension. *International Journal of Research in English Education, 2*(1), 1–7. Retrieved from www.ijreeonline.com

Alber, R. (2014). *6 scaffolding strategies to use with your students.* Retrieved from https://www.edutopia.org/blog/scaffolding-lessons-six-strategies-rebecca-alber

Becker, M., McElvany, N., & Kortenbruck, M. (2010). Intrinsic and extrinsic reading motivation as predictors of reading literacy: A longitudinal study. *Journal of Education Psychology.* Retrieved from https://eric.ed.gov/?id=EJ910431

Cambria, J., & Guthrie, J. T. (2010). Motivating and engaging students in reading. *The NERA Journal, 46(*1), 16–29.

Carroll, J. M., & Fox, A. C. (2017). *Reading self-efficacy predicts word reading but not comprehension in both girls and boys.* Retrieved from https://www.ncbi.nlm.nih.gov/pmc/articles/PMC5239817/

Castle, K. (2015). *Motivation to read: A study of three primary age students.* Retrieved from http://digitalcommons.brockport.edu/cgi/viewcontent.cgi?article=1575&context=ehd_theses

Ciampa, K. (2012). *Reading in the digital age: Using electronic books as a teaching tool for beginning readers.* Retrieved from http://files.eric.ed.gov/fulltext/EJ981797.pdf

Denton, C., & Otaiba, S. (2011). *Teaching word identification to students with reading difficulties and disabilities.* Retrieved from https://www.highbeam.com/doc/1G1-254245149.html

Edmunds, K. M., & Bauserman, K. L. (2006). What teachers can learn about reading motivation through conversations with children. *The Reading Teacher, 59*(5), 414–424. Retrieved from http://www.jstor.org/stable/20204369

Fox, L. C. C. (2014). *Effects of technology on literacy skills and motivation to read and write.* Retrieved from http://digitalcommons.brockport.edu/cgi/viewcontent.cgi?article=1535&context=ehd_theses

Frey, S. (2015). *Study says reading aloud to children, more than talking, builds literacy.* Retrieved from https://edsource.org/2015/study-says-reading-aloud-to-children-morethan-talking-builds-literacy/82045

Froiland, J. M., Oros, E., Smith, L., & Hirchert, T. (2012). Intrinsic motivation to learn: The nexus between psychological health and academic success. *Contemporary School Psychology, 16*, 91–100.

Gambrell, L. (2011). Seven rules of engagement: What's most important to know about motivation to read. *The Reading Teacher, 65*(8), 172–187.

Gambrell, L., & Marinak, B. (2010). *Reading motivation: What the research says.* Retrieved from http://www.readingrockets.org/article/reading-motivation-what-research-says

Guthrie, J. T., & Wigfield, A. (1999). How motivation fits into a science of reading. *Scientific Studies of Reading, 3*, 199–205.

Guthrie, J. T., & Wigfield, A. (2000). Engagement and motivation in reading. In M. L. Kamil, P. B. Mosenthal, P. D. Pearson, & R. Barr (Eds.), *Handbook of reading research* (Vol. 3, pp. 403–422). Mahwah, NJ: Erlbaum.

Guthrie, J. T., Wigfield, A., & You, W. (2012). Instructional contexts for engagement and achievement in reading. In S. Christensen, A. Reschly & C. Wylie (Eds.), Handbook of research on student engagement (pp. 601–634). New York, NY: Springer Science.

Hall, L. (2014). *Examining the relationship between reading ability and reading self-concept in differing socio-economic schools.* Retrieved from http://digitalcommons.uri.edu/cgi/viewcontent.cgi?article=1298&context=theses

Hornery, S., Seaton, M., Tracey, D., Craven, R. G., & Yeung, A. S. (2014). *Enhancing reading skills and reading self-concept of children with reading difficulties: Adopting a dual approach intervention.* Retrieved from http://files.eric.ed.gov/fulltext/EJ1041670.pdf

Hulleman, C. S., Godes, O., Hendricks, G. L., & Harackiewicz, J. M. (2010). Enhancing interest and performance with a utility value intervention. *Journal of Educational Psychology, 102*(4), 880–895. doi:10.1037/ a0019506

Jang, H., Reeve, J., & Deci, E. L. (2010). Engaging students in learning activities: It's not autonomy support or structure, but autonomy support and structure. *Journal of Educational Psychology, 102*, 588-600. DOI: 10.1037/a0019682

McGeown, S., Norgate, R., & Warhurst, A. (2012). Exploring intrinsic and extrinsic reading motivation among very good and very poor readers. *Educational Research, 54*(3), 309–322. doi:10.1080/00131881.2012.710089

Melekoglu, M., & Wilkerson, K. (2013). Motivation to read: How does it change for struggling readers with and without disabilities? *International Journal of Instruction, 6*(1), 77–88.

Morgan, H. (2013). Multimodal children's e-books help young learners in reading. *Early Childhood Education Journal, 41*(6), 477–483. doi:10.1007/s10643-013-0575-8

Provencher, J. (2014, September 24). Car games to improve reading skills [Blog post]. Retrieved from https://www.universitas.ca/en/universitas-blog/car-games-to-improve-reading-skills/

Schaffner, E., Schiefele, U., & Ulferts, H. (2013). Reading amount as a mediator of the effects of intrinsic and extrinsic reading motivation on reading comprehension. *Reading Research Quarterly, 48*(4), 369–385. doi:10.1002/rrq.52

Schiefele, U., Schaffner, E., Möller, J., & Wigfield, A. (2012). Dimensions of reading motivation and their relation to reading behavior and competence. *Reading Research Quarterly, 47*(4), 427–463. doi:10.1002/RRQ.030

Snowling, M. J., & Hulme, C. (2013). Children's reading impairments: From theory to practice. *Japanese Psychological Research, 55*(2), 186–202. doi:10.1111/j.1468-5884.2012.00541.x

Springfield Public Library. (2017). *Storytimes.* Retrieved from http://www.springfieldlibrary.org/library/services/storytimes/

Stanovich, K. E. (1986). Matthew effects in reading: Some consequences of individual differences in the acquisition of literacy. *Reading Research Quarterly, 21*, 360–407.

Strategic Marketing & Research Inc. (2013). *Factors affecting reading ability in school age children.* Retrieved from http://www.evancedsolutions.com/wpcontent/uploads/2015/01/Factors_Affecting_Reading_Ability_White_Paper.pdf

Torres, K. (2010). *Factors that influence students' motivation to read across grade levels.* Retrieved from http://fisherpub.sjfc.edu/cgi/viewcontent.cgi?article=1002&context=education_ETD_masters

U.S. Department of Education. (2016). *The condition of education 2016: Home literacy activities with young children.* Retrieved from https://nces.ed.gov/programs/coe/indicator_sfa.asp

Chapter Four

Designing Successful Reading Comprehension Programs

Promising Instructional Strategies and Practices

Nicholas D. Young and
Kristen Bonanno-Sotiropoulos

Reading comprehension difficulties are among the most significant problems experienced by children identified with learning disabilities (LD). This is because reading comprehension underlies their performance in the majority of academic domains, as well as their adjustments to most school activities (Kang, McKenna, Arden, and Ciullo, 2015; National Center for Education Statistics, 2011). The National Reading Panel was commissioned in 1997 through the National Institute of Child Health and Human Development and was charged with identifying evidence through extensive research of best practices for teaching children how to read.

The executive report by the National Reading Panel (2000) identified the critical areas that students need to demonstrate proficiency in order to become effective readers. These areas include phonemic awareness, phonics, fluency, vocabulary development, and reading comprehension. The executive report stressed that a combination of best instructional approaches are most beneficial. Teaching techniques that include explicit, or direct, instruction in phonemic awareness, systematic phonics instruction, guided oral reading practice, and vocabulary instruction, as well as strategies for reading comprehension are most effective when used in conjunction with each other.

A synthesis of current research conducted by Kim, Linan-Thompson, and Misquitta (2012) revealed five critical components for increasing reading comprehension for students with LD. Among the five are: the type of instructional methods, development of self-monitoring skills, the incorporation of various reading components within an intervention, the fidelity of the instruction provided, and the size of the instructional group.

Strickland, Boon, and Spencer (2013) further examined the research on the effects of repeated reading interventions on reading comprehension and fluency for students with LD. Their findings indicated that repeated reading interventions do in fact increase both fluency and comprehension; however, this was only significant on practiced readings and did not significantly generalize to new texts.

Hall (2015) harmonized a body of research looking at inference strategies for struggling readers as well as students with LD. She concluded that the most effective inference interventions included instruction in the following areas: activating prior knowledge, integration of prior knowledge into current reading, identification of key words or clues, using key words in answering inferencing questions, and conducting interventions in small groups or one to one.

Two valuable instructional strategies for increasing reading comprehension for students with LD, direct and strategy instructional approaches, are frequently referenced practices in the literature. Both direct and strategy instructional practices should work in harmony in order to create and provide the ideal learning opportunities to increase a student's comprehension levels. Several effective intervention strategies, such as repeated readings, story mapping, and the use of graphic organizers, combine both direct and strategy instructional approaches and offer beneficial results.

DIRECT AND STRATEGY INSTRUCTIONAL APPROACHES FOR INCREASING READING COMPREHENSION

Gersten et al. (2001) highlight the importance of strategy instruction in the area of reading comprehension. The theoretical model behind several reading comprehension studies relates to strategy instruction. Strategy instruction refers to the teaching of rules, routines, and procedures for students to develop, practice, and independently utilize when reading text (Kamil et al., 2008). Strategy instruction interventions, which combine goal setting and process approaches, have been shown to produce moderate to large effect sizes (Gillespie & Graham, 2014).

Although direct and strategy instruction treatments may be distinguished by the unit of information (i.e., direct instruction focuses primarily on isolated skills, whereas strategy instruction focuses primarily on rules) and processing perspective (i.e., direct instruction is characterized as a bottom-up processing approach and strategy instruction as a top-down processing approach), there are, of course, other distinctions that are less subtle. These distinctions can be sorted into various categories. For example, direct instruction emphasizes fast-paced, well-sequenced, and highly focused lessons.

Direct instruction usually occurs in small student groups where learners are given several opportunities to respond to and receive feedback about accuracy and responses (Edmonds et al., 2009; Kim et al., 2012). A comprehensive review of strategy instruction program literature by several pundits (Lenhard, Baier, Endlich, Schneider, & Hoffmann, 2013; Wanzek, Wexler, Vaughn, & Ciullo, 2010) showcases the importance of specific instructional components:

- Advanced organizers: providing students with a type of mental scaffolding on which to build new understanding
- Organization: directing students to stop from time to time to assess their understanding
- Elaboration: thinking about the material to be learned in a way that connects the material to information or ideas already in their mind
- Generative learning: making sense of what they are learning by summarizing the information
- General study strategies: underlining, note taking, summarizing, having students generate questions, outlining, and working in pairs to summarize sections of materials
- Metacognition: thinking about and controlling one's thinking process
- Attributions: evaluating the effectiveness of a strategy

CRITICAL COMPONENTS IN DEVELOPING AN EFFECTIVE READING COMPREHENSION PROGRAM STRATEGY INSTRUCTION

A large amount of research supports the effectiveness of strategy instruction to increase reading comprehension skills for students with LD. Specifically, teaching strategies for finding main idea and summarizing skills are critical components. According to Kamil et al. (2008), "Struggling adolescent readers need direct, explicit instruction in comprehension strategies to improve their reading comprehension" (par. 1). Comprehension teaching strategies should include techniques for summarizing; asking and answering questions, including "wh" questions; identifying the main idea; and approaches for paraphrasing.

In Pursuit of a Balanced Instructional Approach

Beyond strategy teaching, modeling self-monitoring concepts, active student participation, scaffolding techniques, and both guided practice and opportunities for independent practice should all be an integral part of any reading intervention program (Kamil et al., 2008). A balanced instructional approach compared to simply focused instruction has yielded higher outcomes as well. For example, combining vocabulary instruction into comprehension strategies would prove beneficial for students with LD.

At the secondary level, Watson, Gable, Gear, and Hughes (2012) compiled a summary of evidenced-based strategies for improving reading comprehension for students with LD. Among the most valuable are activating prior knowledge, supporting and increasing student motivation, and explicitly teaching vocabulary, text coherence, and text structure. In addition to the strategies referenced here, the incorporation of peer-mentoring or peer-mediated interventions have been associated with positive growth in both reading and writing for students with LD (Kaldenberg, Watt, & Therrien, 2014).

Size of Instructional Grouping Matters

Small-group instruction is vital to the success to any reading comprehension program for students with LD (Kim et al., 2012). Smaller group ratios increase the likelihood of academic success by offering increased teacher-student interactions, individualized instruction, increased student engagement, consistent student progress monitoring, and opportunities for frequent feedback (Vaughn et al., 2003; Vaughn & Wanzek, 2014).

Vaughn et al. (2003) concluded that smaller instructional groupings had better student outcomes for students with reading difficulties. Specifically, groups of either 1:1 (one teacher to one student) or 1:3 (one teacher to three students) showed greater positive gains than groups of 1:10 (one teacher to ten students) or larger. In addition, the authors determined that instructional groupings of a 1:3 ratio proved most beneficial for English language learners (ELLs). Instructional groupings of 1:3 provide ELLs with not only direct teacher instruction but peer-modeling opportunities and peer interaction as well.

INTERVENTION STRATEGIES FOR INCREASING READING COMPREHENSION

Intensive Reading Interventions

Vaughn and Wanzek (2014) presented a strong rationale for more explicit teaching as a means of increasing reading development in students with LD. A large discrepancy was identified in the time that students were engaged in the task of reading within general education classrooms, specifically students with LD. This comes at an important time in educational reform when most students with disabilities are receiving instruction within inclusive classrooms. Prior to 1990, students with disabilities were receiving extensively more individualized or small-group instruction (Vaughn & Wanzek, 2014). Within the last several years, small-group instruction within the general education classroom has become more common.

Vaughn and Wanzek (2014) also assert that superior reading instruction for students with disabilities must encompass three components: quality reading instruction, small-group or individual instruction, and extended duration of the intervention. Quality of reading instruction assures that special education teachers have the proper training and resources they need to provide intensive interventions. As stated previously, research has supported the effectiveness of small-group or individual intensive instruction for students with LD (Vaughn et al., 2003). Intensive instruction conducted in this manner allows for explicit teaching of the critical elements of reading, as well as providing abundant opportunities for immediate feedback, practice, and risk taking.

Graphic Organizers and Story Mapping Techniques

Graphic organizers are assistive tools that help students organize information in order to comprehend concepts. Graphic organizers help to empower students to become engaged learners. In relation to increasing reading comprehension, Watson et al. (2012) describe graphic organizers as providing students with "a cognitive structure, a framework to relate existing knowledge to new information to be learned" (p. 83). The use of graphic organizers provides students with a conceptual image of what it is they are reading or learning.

The use of graphic organizers can play a role in activating a learner's schema, and therefore assist with connecting ideas. The use of graphic organizers also allows for the quick retrieval of information or reading elements to assist with comprehension and therefore prevents taxing working memory overload. By decreasing such overload, students have the ability to better use their cognitive resources to comprehend and make connections.

An example of using graphic organizers in reading comprehension interventions is known as story mapping or story grammar. Story grammar essentially refers to story mapping through the use of graphic organizers. When students are using story grammar strategies they utilize graphic organizers to identify the various elements within a narrative. Story elements refer to such things as characters, setting, the problem, and so forth. Story grammar strategies involve three critical phases. The first, referred to as modeling, involves the teacher explicitly teaching the strategy.

It is important that the teacher discuss the different narrative elements, and model how to identify the elements within a narrative and how to transfer those elements onto the story map (Alves, Kennedy, Brown, & Solis, 2015). The second phase, guided practice, allows the students to practice what they have learned while receiving support from the teacher and their peers. The final phase, independent practice, engages the students in individual practice from start to finish (Kaldenberg et al., 2014; Wanzek & Kent, 2012).

Repeated Reading Interventions: How Effective Are They?

Repeated reading interventions assist with increasing reading fluency and the development of reading comprehension (Strickland et al., 2013). During repeated reading interventions, a student will silently listen to a teacher or peer read aloud a short passage. The teacher or peer will model appropriate fluency, speed, accuracy, and expression. The student will then read the passage over and over until he or she has reached a level of satisfactory fluency.

During the reading, students can ask for help with sounding out words. As students move to higher grades, comprehension questions can be added in. Repeated reading interventions are very easy to implement and do not require much planning time. In addition, there is little teacher training needed and passages can be easily adapted to fit curricular content (Strickland et al., 2013). As a result, many teachers may turn to this type of intervention.

Following an extensive review of repeated reading practices for students with LD, Strickland et al. (2013) concluded that significant gains related to practice readings only and were minor to moderate when generalized to new passages. This suggests that the use of repeated reading practice holds some promise but should be used in combination with other reading interventions.

Inferencing Instruction

Part of reading comprehension involves the ability to make inferences. When individuals read, they make connections to prior knowledge, other readings, or real-world experiences. This coherence in meaningful connections provides the basis for making inferences. The ability to make inferences is "multifaceted and requires the orchestration of skills that pose problems for those with disabilities" (Reed & Lynn, 2016, p. 133). Inferencing requires multiple cognition means: accessing prior knowledge, retaining new information, and the ability to stay focused and attend to the tasks at hand.

Hall (2015) examined a vast body of research specifically focused on effective inferencing teaching strategies for struggling readers as well as students with LD. She concluded that the most effective inference interventions included instruction in the following: activating prior knowledge, integration of prior knowledge into current reading, identification of key words or clues, and using these key words in answering inferencing questions, as well as conducting interventions in small groups or one to one.

Reed and Lynn (2016) also looked at inferencing interventions and discovered that teaching inferencing skills along with self-regulation skills and goal-setting skills proved to generate better learning outcomes. The authors found this to be very successful with middle school students with LD. The ideas presented by many pundits (Alves et al., 2015; Hall, 2015; Kaldenberg et al., 2014; Vaughn & Wanzek, 2014; Watson et al., 2012) support the idea of activating prior knowledge, preteaching key vocabulary, and the use of graphic organizers to assist with reading comprehension for students with LD.

CONCLUSION

Research has identified five critical program components necessary for increasing reading comprehension, including the type of instructional methods, development of self-monitoring skills, the incorporation of various reading components within an intervention, the fidelity of the instruction provided, as well as the size of the instructional group (Kamil et al., 2008; Kim et al., 2012; Watson et al., 2012).

While instructional approaches have been the focus of this chapter, the importance of instructional groupings should not be overlooked in pursuit of more cost-effective alternatives. Small-group instruction is vital to the success of any reading comprehension program for students with LD (Kim et al., 2012). This is because they provide increased opportunities for student and teacher interactions, immediate feedback, active engagement, and peer interaction (Vaughn et al., 2003; Vaughn & Wanzek, 2014).

Repeated reading fluency interventions have been shown to result in some positive gains but are most effective when combined with other evidenced-based strategies (Strickland et al., 2013). Reed and Lynn (2016) further underscore the potency of teaching inferencing instruction, coupled with self-regulation and goal-setting skills, to improve reading comprehension program outcomes.

POINTS TO REMEMBER

- Reading comprehension difficulties are among the most significant problems for students identified as having a learning disability. This affects learning in all content areas.
- The five critical components to increasing reading comprehension for students with learning disabilities include: the type of instructional method, development of self-monitoring skills, the integration of various reading components and strategies into any reading intervention program, fidelity in the instruction provided, and the size of the instructional group.

- Effective comprehension and inferencing interventions should include strategies for activating prior knowledge, strategies to incorporate prior knowledge into current reading tasks, explicit teaching of vocabulary and key words, incorporating instruction in self-monitoring and self-regulation skills, and small-group or one-to-one instruction.
- The use of graphic organizers has proven highly effective in increasing reading comprehension. Graphic organizers prevent working memory overload and provide students with a conceptual image of what they are reading and quick retrieval of facts, and they therefore increase comprehension.

REFERENCES

Alves, K., Kennedy, M., Brown, T., & Solis, M. (2015). Story grammar instruction with third and fifth grade students with LD and other struggling readers. *LD: A Contemporary Journal, 13*(1), 73–93.

Edmonds, M. S., Vaughn, S., Wexler, J., Reutebuch, C., Cable, A., Tackett, K. K., & Schnakenberg, J. W. (2009). A synthesis of reading interventions and effects on reading comprehension outcomes for older struggling readers. *Review of Educational Research, 79*(1), 262–300.

Gersten, R., Fuchs, L. S., Williams, J. P., & Baker, S. (2001). Teaching reading comprehension strategies to students with learning disabilities: A review of the research. *Review of Educational Research*. Retrieved from http://edci6300introresearch.pbworks.com/f/Gersten+et+al+2001+reading+comprehension+leanring+disabilities.pdf

Gillespie, A., and Graham, S. (2014). A meta-analysis of writing interventions for students with learning disabilities. *Exceptional Children, 80*(4), 454–473.

Hall, C. (2015). Inference instruction for struggling readers: A synthesis of intervention research. *Educational Psychology Review*. Springer Science Business Media. New York.

Kaldenberg, E., Watt, S., and Therrien, W. (2014). Reading instruction in science for students with learning disabilities: A meta-analysis. *Learning Disabilities Quarterly, 38*(3), 160–173.

Kamil, M. L., Borman, G. D., Dole, J., Kral, C. C., Salinger, T., and Torgesen, J. (2008). *Improving adolescent literacy: Effective classroom and intervention practices; A practice guide* (NCEE #2008-4027). Washington, DC: National Center for Education Evaluation and Regional Assistance, Institute of Education Sciences, U.S. Department of Education. Retrieved from http://ies.ed.gov/ncee/wwc

Kang, E. Y., McKenna, J., Arden, S., and Ciullo, S. (2015). Integrated reading and writing interventions for students with learning disabilities: A review of the literature. *Learning Disabilities Research & Practice, 31*(1), 22–33.

Kim, W., Linan-Thompson, S., and Misquitta, R. (2012). Critical factors in reading comprehension instruction for students with LD: A research synthesis. *LD Research Practice, 27*(2), 66–78.

Lenhard, W., Baier, H., Endlich, D., Schneider, W., & Hoffmann, J. (2013). Rethinking strategy instruction: Direct reading strategy instruction versus computer-based guided practice. *Journal of Research in Reading, 36*(2), 223–240. doi:10.1111/j.1467-9817.2011.01505.x

National Center for Education Statistics. (2011). *The national report card: Institute of Education Sciences (IES)*. Washington, DC. Department of Education.

National Reading Panel. (2000). *Teaching children to read: An evidence-based assessment of the scientific research literature on reading and its implications for reading instruction.* Washington, DC: U.S. Government Printing Office.

Reed, D., and Lynn, D. (2016). The effects of an inference-making strategy taught with and without goal setting. *LD Quarterly, 39*(3), 133–145.

Strickland, W., Boon, R., and Spencer, V. (2013). The effects of repeated reading on the fluency and comprehension skills of elementary-age students with Learning Disabilities (LD), 2001–2011: A review of research and practice. *LD: A Contemporary Journal, 11*(1), 1–33.

Vaughn, S., Linan-Thompson, S., Kouzekanani, K., Bryant D., Dickson, S., and Blozis, S. (2003). Reading instruction grouping for students with reading difficulties. *Remedial and Special Education, 24*(5), 301–315.

Vaughn, S., & Wanzek, J. (2014). Intensive interventions in reading for students with reading disabilities: Meaningful impacts. *LD Research & Practice, 29*(2), 46–53.

Wanzek, J., & Kent, S. (2012). Reading interventions for students with learning disabilities in the upper elementary grades. *LD: A Contemporary Journal, 10*(1), 5–16.

Wanzek, J., Wexler, J., Vaughn, S., and Ciullo, S. (2010). Reading interventions for struggling readers in the upper elementary grades: A synthesis of 20 years of research. *Reading and Writing, 23*, 889–912.

Watson, S., Gable, R., Gear, S., and Hughes, K. (2012). Evidence-based strategies for improving the reading comprehension of secondary students: Implications for students with LD. *LD Research & Practice, 27*(2), 79–89.

Chapter Five

Reading in the Twenty-First Century

Utilizing Digital Literacy Practices and Assessments to Help Struggling Secondary Readers

Nicholas D. Young and Melissa A. Mumby

Student learning in the twenty-first century has changed dramatically. With so much information available at the touch of a button, students are exposed to more learning opportunities than ever before (Hayes Jacobs, 2010). Yet surprisingly, many schools are slow to adopt practices that reach the multiple ways in which students learn best (Reeves, 2007).

Two decades ago, in 1997, the National Reading Panel was formed at the request of Congress to investigate the ways in which children were learning to read, along with strategies that could best help support an effective reading program (National Institute of Child Health and Human Development [NICHD], 2016). Not surprisingly, the panel found that there was not much research into the use of computers in reading education, citing only twenty-one studies at the time. However, out of those studies, they all reported positive results from engaging the use of computers in reading instruction (NICHD, 2016).

There is an emerging body of research that suggests educators must design practices that assess the multiple ways in which students learn in order to create a level playing field for all students, especially in the area of reading and literacy (Hayes Jacobs, 2010). Studies show that educators who embrace teaching to students' multiple intelligences, often through the use of technology, can help students to become more successful than through traditional teaching practices alone (Best & Dunlap, 2012; Hayes Jacobs, 2014; Hoerr, 1994; Samur, 2011; Stanford, 2003).

It would seem, then, that educators who are invested in seeing their students succeed on a global level would be quick to incorporate these practices into their daily lessons. Yet, many educators and educational leaders are unsure of the longevity of these new practices, and if there is truly a necessity to break away from practices that have been historically successful for the majority of learners (Best & Dunlap, 2012).

Not surprisingly, when working with students of all ability levels, studies show that the more varied techniques used in the classroom, the better the outcome for all learners (Hayes Jacobs, 2014; Jacobs, 2013; Reeves, 2007; Stanford, 2003; Voltz, Sims, & Nelson, 2010). Students who are identified as learning disabled, or LD, are growing in numbers. According to the National Center for Education Statistics (2016), the overall number of students served in federally supported special education programs rose from 8.3 percent in the 1976–1977 school year, to 12.9 percent in the 2013–2014 school year.

Much of this increase is arguably due to the qualification of students under the category of specific learning disabilities, which rose from 1.8 percent in the 1976–1977 school year to 4.5 percent in the 2013–2014 school year. Students who are labeled as LD are not only challenged by school curriculum, but also by the growing demands of a world that requires rapid thought processing and reasoning skills, along with the increased ability to read complex information (Flores, Matkin, Burbach, Quinn, & Harding, 2012).

Perhaps most concerning is that students who cannot master the basics of reading are likely to have low self-esteem, diminished self-worth, and a desire to drop out of school (Lyons, 2003). In order to tap into a child's ability to successfully learn to read and write, educators must focus first on motivation. Lyons (2003) explains that motivation is a state of mind that a student must activate for him- or herself; it is not something that a teacher or parent can give to a child or create for a student. Challenge is necessary to stimulate the desire to learn. When children are presented with new challenges that they can surmount, they develop a belief in themselves that they can learn and achieve (Hayes Jacobs, 2010; Lyons, 2003).

Providing appropriate levels of challenge to students is key to creating individuals who have strong self-esteem and feelings of self-worth. This is especially true for students at the secondary level. While many high school–aged students still struggle with basic decoding skills, more prevalent is the number of students who cannot comprehend what they are reading (Lyons, 2003).

According to research presented by the U.S. Department of Education (2015), the National Assessment of Educational Progress (NAEP) reading assessment showed a decline in the area of reading comprehension among twelfth-grade students between 1992 and 2015. Overall, only 37 percent of these students were reading at or above the proficiency level. While this statistic varied by subgroup, the data is concerning in the aggregate. One may argue that this decline in proficiency comes from a change in reading culture, and the values held by the majority of students with regard to reading for multiple purposes.

While it's true that all culture is educative, it's the way in which educators tap into that culture that makes it an effective teaching and learning tool (Sandlin, Wright, & Clark, 2011). Included in that approach comes the necessity to design curriculum and assessments that address all the ways in which students demonstrate mastery (Hayes Jacobs, 2010; Hoerr, 1994; Samur, 2011; Wolfe, 2010).

Looking forward to the types of skills students will need as they navigate the twenty-first century, educators must tap into the available technology in order to create ways of assessing students' reading skills that align with global demands, specifically in the area of learning to read for information (Hayes Jacobs, 2010). In other words, students must now become digitally literate in order to be competitive in the twenty-first-century workforce (Best & Dunlap, 2012). Yet one question remains: How should educators go about combining technology with teaching in order to help students to better comprehend what they read? More specifically, is it possible to utilize the ways in which students already access technology as a basis for developing stronger reading comprehension skills?

DEFINING DIGITAL LITERACY

Digital literacy has been widely defined to include a range of activities such as enrolling in online courses to completing very basic educational activities on a classroom computer (Best & Dunlap, 2012). Because students live their lives in a digital world that provides constant information at their fingertips, it is necessary for educators to set parameters for the ways in which students should correctly utilize digital tools and media (Best & Dunlap, 2012; Hayes Jacobs, 2010, 2014).

Hayes Jacobs (2014) suggests that there are four actions that support what it means to be digitally literate in the educative sense:

1. Students need the skills to access the Internet. Students need entry points into the digital world, such as a basic understanding of technological terminology, as well as keyboarding skills.
2. Students need to be taught how to selectively judge the quality of websites and other applications to ensure that the information obtained is correct.

3. A student must take those quality sites and preserve them for future use, perhaps through the creation of their own websites, or through regular interaction with a classroom website.
4. Students must be responsible for showcasing their work in a digital format, such as maintaining a digital portfolio, or through application creation programs where students can create their own innovative applications.

As students are able to move from the basic to the advanced, educators are given the opportunity to develop much more progressive methods in the classroom (Samur, 2011).

INTEGRATING NEW TECHNOLOGY INTO THE CLASSROOM

In order to effectively integrate new technology into educational practice and successfully use it to help struggling readers, teachers must be able to reflect upon the ways in which technology-centered practices challenge today's students (Wiske, Franz, & Breit, 2005). It is not enough to incorporate one or two pieces of technology into the classroom on a sporadic basis; students must be able to utilize this technology to develop a deep understanding of curricular material, while becoming more efficient learners (Wiske et al., 2005).

One way to ensure that the use of technology is effective for its intended purpose is to consider multiple intelligence (MI) theory when thinking of ways in which to incorporate new technology into the classroom. Multiple intelligence theory suggests that learners fit into multiple categories of learning abilities (Gardner, 1997). This theory essentially suggests that no one set of strategies works best for all students at all times, and that educators should set out to touch upon as many of the intelligences as possible in the course of both lessons and assessments (Stanford, 2003).

In thinking about helping struggling readers, it is important to remember that reading does not have to be a practice in which a student merely sits with a book and decodes words. Reading can be dynamic, and oftentimes students who are taught using multifaceted approaches are more likely to develop strategies that help them make sense of new and challenging text (Shelby-Caffey, Ubeda, & Jenkins, 2014).

While it is not realistic to expect to use all of the intelligences in a lesson, it is important to recognize the need for diversity when it comes to presentation (Jacobs, 2013; Reeves, 2007; Stanford, 2003). That being said, the use of digital technology in the classroom makes it easier to reach students that have previously been underserved by more traditional teaching methods (Hayes Jacobs, 2010; Monroe, 2004).

Stanford (2003) suggests that "unsuccessful, unmotivated students have experienced academic growth when exposed to multifaceted interventions and techniques principled by MI theory" (p. 81). Unfortunately, traditional teaching methods often place too much emphasis on practices with which many students have marked difficulty, such as listening to lectures or participating in timed writing activities.

For struggling readers, especially those at the secondary level of their school careers, traditional teaching methodology proves problematic for several reasons, chiefly because students who have not been successful learning to read early in life are less likely to become motivated to try (Lyons, 2003). Updated curriculum practices must support the creation of dynamic lessons that focus on motivating students to want to master reading as a skill (Voltz et al., 2010).

In order to cover curriculum and prepare for the twenty-first-century workforce, it is vital that students become flexible thinkers, problem solvers, and readers. Wiske et al. (2005) argue that students become better able to adapt to changing local and global needs through increasing their ability to demonstrate their knowledge as either product or performance; however, it is not always clear how this is to be accomplished. In a time when reading for information is critical to an individual's understanding of the world, it is crucial to develop multiple strategies for which this is to be accomplished (Shelby-Caffey et al., 2014).

This is where the need for classroom technology becomes critical to the type of well-rounded education needed for global competitiveness. For all students to benefit from an increase in technology use within the classroom, educators must be willing to not only change their teaching strategies and curricula, but also create assessments that align with twenty-first-century standards (Stanford, 2003). Hayes Jacobs (2014) argues that educators must "concentrate on deliberately shifting and upgrading curriculum assessment and instruction . . . with contemporary approaches that achieve the sort of deep learning that research says matters most" (p. 62).

Moving toward a twenty-first-century design for teaching and learning does not simply come from outfitting schools with more computers. It is the ability for teachers to utilize these tools in ways that make the curriculum accessible to all students that creates a well-rounded learning environment. Research has shown that technology can help prepare students for the workforce on a global level (Best & Dunlap, 2012). Yet, in order for students to benefit from increased technology use in the classroom, educators must first teach students how to use that technology in ways that are meaningful.

Classrooms that embrace a computer-supported collaborative learning (CSCL) environment are often at the forefront of achievement gains for underperforming students (Samur, 2011). CSCL environments allow students to tap into their multiple intelligences, while learning how to work interactively, as well as to make decisions based on the interests of a group (Samur, 2011).

These classrooms offer much more than collaboration; they allow students to learn how to use technology from a very basic level, such as the development of keyboarding skills, all the way up to more advanced practices, including creating web pages and editing wikis, while reinforcing higher-order analytical skills through the analysis of information quality (Hayes Jacobs, 2014; Samur, 2011).

Becoming media literate is a necessity of the twenty-first century, since most students are more apt to "read" the Internet or get their information from television than from a book or newspaper (Hayes Jacobs, 2014). By affording students the opportunity to become more discerning users of technology, so, too, are students becoming more actively engaged with all forms of media. The goal of digital and media literacy is to challenge students' notions of what it means to be a consumer of technology, as well as what it means to analyze information (Hayes Jacobs, 2010, 2014).

ASSESSING READING COMPREHENSION USING DIGITAL TECHNOLOGY

Media and digital literacy allows students to engage with a variety of new texts. Adlington and Hansford (2008) argue that texts are no longer experienced as singular artifacts, but rather as multimodal experiences with which students can become involved. For example, many of today's most popular print-based books have been turned into films, interactive computer games, and even smartphone applications.

Educators must be able to access these constructs as a means in which to provide students with ways to reflect and create new meaning (Sørensen & Levinsen, 2015). In this way, students are able to "achieve a broader repertoire through which to experience the world and express themselves while learning" (Sørensen & Levinsen, 2015, p. 291).

According to Hayes Jacobs (2014), the goal of forward-thinking assessment practices is to ensure that students become "globally literate." Students who are globally literate can investigate the world through the use of technology, can recognize perspectives of people both within and outside of their own culture, are able to communicate ideas effectively across the globe, and can take action on matters that affect them both locally and globally (Hayes Jacobs, 2014).

Currently, however, most educators only assess students on the most basic of concepts. A glimpse at most state standardized exams shows that students are mainly assessed on their ability to read, answer questions about a reading selection, and compose short answers and essays using textual evidence. This often proves difficult for students who struggle with reading comprehension and who lack the motivation to become better at the skill. Changes in assessment practices that focus on more cutting-edge approaches will, no doubt, positively influence student performance (Hayes Jacobs, 2014).

MODELS OF ASSESSING READING COMPREHENSION THROUGH DIGITAL PRACTICES: A SNAPSHOT

What do some of these innovative assessments look like? Taking into account Gardner's multiple intelligences theory, reading assessment should be multimodal, and these assessments should be formatted in ways in which students can show mastery in myriad ways (Best & Dunlap, 2012; Voltz et al., 2010).

Research has shown that the more the assessment tool can be manipulated, the greater the student achievement (Adlington & Hansford, 2008; Adsanatham, 2012; Best & Dunlap, 2012; Hayes Jacobs, 2014; Jacobs, 2013; Samur, 2011; Sørensen & Levinsen, 2015). There are several examples in the research that show innovative ways with which to assess student mastery in reading and writing. However, they all share the common bond of being digital and multimodal in nature.

One of the most popular, trendsetting methods of assessment in digital education is the wiki. Wikis are Internet spaces where all people can write and edit the same document, which allows them to express unique ideas, explore others' ideas, and move toward collaboration with people from around the world (Samur, 2011). The use of wikis in the classroom presents students with the opportunity to communicate ideas in an asynchronous environment, without time or location barriers.

Wikis are essentially living documents in which students can add, delete, or change information based on what they are learning in the classroom. These spaces also function to teach interpersonal skills such as listening and respecting others' opinions, collaborating on group tasks, and increasing communication skills (Samur, 2011). Another benefit of using a wiki as an assessment tool is that educators can track a student's progress over time. Educators can assess the student's progress in writing, evaluating information, and communication, for example (Samur, 2011).

Using digital technology to assess concept mastery also affords students the opportunity to create their own grading criteria (Adsanatham, 2012). Because digital assessment is new and unique, the criteria on which student achievement is determined must be tailored to fit the assessment medium. Allowing students to develop rubrics around their own mastery gives students agency over their own learning (Adsanatham, 2012).

There must be a framework into which the student-developed outline will fit. For example, students who are studying narrative using an interactive game model should be able to demonstrate an understanding of the ways in which shared meanings connect people on a social level (Jacobs, 2013). Similarly, students should be able to explain how their understanding fits into the larger world of meaning, or context (Jacobs, 2013). In this way, students are able to demonstrate a newly developed knowledge base that connects them to a more globalized standard of learning.

Educators should see these new ways of assessing as not mere add-ons to the existing curriculum, but instead as an integral part of the development of a hybrid pedagogy, where old basics and new technologies are intertwined (Jacobs, 2013). While new assessment techniques will certainly have their challenges, they can be incredibly helpful in determining student readiness for the twenty-first-century workforce (Adsanatham, 2012).

CONCLUSION

While the use of digital technology to help struggling readers has its critics, there is little doubt that this emerging practice will become relevant for educators who are trying to determine the best ways to reach their students in an increasingly technologically driven society. The use of new technologies creates the potential to reach multitudes of students who have historically been unable to attend to the material being taught in the classroom (Kop & Hill, 2008).

As educators begin to readily adopt multifaceted teaching strategies that focus on technology, student performance in the area of reading comprehension and reading for information will likely increase (Hayes Jacobs, 2014). There is a paradigm shift occurring in education, and in order to keep up with the trends of present and future, it a critical to think outside the box and meet students in the world in which they feel most comfortable (Bell, 2011; Kropf, 2013; Ravenscroft, 2011).

POINTS TO REMEMBER

- Teaching and learning has changed dramatically in the twenty-first century, and students are more likely to go to the Internet for their information than pick up a book or newspaper.
- An early study from the National Reading Panel suggested that the use of computers in reading instruction had a consistently positive impact on student performance.
- One way to reach struggling readers who lack the motivation to become better at the skill is to tap into digital technology to create learning envi-

ronments and lessons that are dynamic. Students who are able to participate in reading as a multimodal experience are more likely to maintain
interest, as well as show increases in performance.

* Digital literacy refers to a multitude of practices that include the use of
technology in the classroom, from very basic computing skills, to the
creation of web pages and other digital products. Students who are able to
demonstrate their learning as either performance or product are more likely to be invested in the outcome.

* Reading comprehension and literacy are multifaceted skills that require
outside-the-box thinking in order to reach students who have grown up in
a technologically driven society.

* Assessment practices involving digital literacy must be designed in ways
that connect with students' multiple intelligences. Reading comprehension
can be measured through a student's ability to evaluate and formulate
opinions on information, in addition to sharing what he or she has learned
with others.

REFERENCES

Adlington, R., & Hansford, D. (2008, July). *Digital spaces and young people's online author-
ing: Challenges for teachers.* Paper presented at the National Conference for Teachers of
English Literacy, Adelaide, Australia.

Adsanatham, C. (2012). Integrating assessment and instruction: Using student-generated grading criteria to evaluate multimodal digital projects. *Computers and Composition, 29,*
152–174.

Bell, F. (2011). Connectivism: Its place in theory-informed research and innovation in technol-
ogy-enabled learning. *International Review of Research in Open and Distance Learning,
12*(3), 98–118.

Best, J., & Dunlap, A. (2012). Beyond access: Effective digital learning for a globalized world.
Mid-Continent Research for Education and Learning. Retrieved from http://files.eric.ed.
gov/fulltext/ED544254.pdf

Flores, K. L., Matkin, G. S., Burbach, M. E., Quinn, C. E., & Harding, H. (2012). Deficient
critical thinking skills among college graduates: Implications for leadership. *Educational
Philosophy and Theory, 44*(2), 213–230. doi:10.1111/j.1469-5812.2010.00672.x

Gardner, H. (1997). Multiple intelligence as a partner in school improvement. *Educational
Leadership, 55*(1), 20–21.

Hayes Jacobs, H. (Ed.). (2010). *Curriculum 21: Essential education for a changing world.*
Alexandria, VA: ASCD.

Hayes Jacobs, H. (2014). Activating digital-media-global literacies & learning. *Independent
School,* 60–68. Retrieved from http://nhje.plymouth.edu/?article=activating-digital-
mediaglobal-literacies-and-learning

Hoerr, T. (1994). How the New City School applies the multiple intelligences. *Educational
Leadership, 52*(3), 29–33.

Jacobs, G. E. (2013). Designing assessments: A multiliteracies approach. *Journal of Adolescent
& Adult Literacy, 56*(8), 623–626.

Kop, R., & Hill, A. (2008). Connectivism: Learning theory of the future or vestige of the past?
International Review of Research in Open and Distance Learning, 9(3), 1–13.

Kropf, D. (2013). Connectivism: 21st century's new learning theory. *European Journal of
Open Distance, and e-Learning, 16*(2), 13–24.

Lyons, C. A. (2003). *Teaching struggling readers: How to use brain-based research to maximize learning.* Portsmouth, NH: Heinemann.

Monroe, B. (2004). *Crossing the digital divide: Race, writing, and technology in the classroom.* New York, NY: Teachers College Press.

National Center for Education Statistics. (2016). *Fast facts: Students with disabilities.* U.S. Department of Education, Institute of Education Science. Retrieved from http://nces.ed.gov/fastfacts/display.asp?id=64

National Institute of Child Health and Human Development (2016). *National reading panel.* Retrieved from https://www.nichd.nih.gov/research/supported/Pages/nrp.aspx

Ravenscroft, A. (2011). Dialogue and connectivism: A new approach to understanding and promoting dialogue-rich networked learning. *International Review of Research in Open and Distance Learning, 12*(3), 139–160.

Reeves, D. (Ed.). (2007). *Ahead of the curve: The power of assessment to transform teaching and learning.* Bloomington, IN: Solution Tree.

Samur, M. Y. (2011). Using wikis as a support and assessment tool in collaborative digital game-based learning environments. *Turkish Online Journal of Distance Education, 12*(2), 70–75.

Sandlin J. A., Wright, R. R., & Clark, C. (2011). Reexamining theories of adult learning and adult development through the lenses of public pedagogy. *Adult Education Quarterly, 63*(1), 3–23. doi:10.1177/0741713611415836

Shelby-Caffey, C., Úbéda, E., & Jenkins, B. (2014). Digital storytelling revisited: An educator's use of an innovative literacy practice. *Reading Teacher, 68*(3), 191–199.

Sørensen, B. H., & Levinsen, K. T. (2015). Powerful practices in digital learning processes. *Electronic Journal of e-Learning, 13*(4), 291–301.

Stanford, P. (2003). Multiple intelligence for every classroom. *Intervention in school and clinic, 39*(2), 80–85.

U.S. Department of Education (2015). *The nation's report card.* Retrieved from https://www.nationsreportcard.gov/reading_math_g12_2015/#reading

Voltz, D. L., Sims, M. J., & Nelson, B. (2010). *Connecting teachers, students, and standards: Strategies for success in diverse and inclusive classrooms.* Alexandria, VA: ASCD.

Wiske, M. S., Franz, K. R., & Breit, L. (2005). *Teaching for understanding with technology.* San Francisco, CA: Jossey-Bass.

Wolfe, P. (2010). *Brain matters: Translating research into classroom practices* (2nd ed.). Alexandria, VA: ASCD.

Chapter Six

Using Peer-Assisted Strategies to Reverse Matthew Effects in Reading

Paul L. Morgan, Caresa Young, Doug Fuchs, and
Kristen Bonanno-Sotiropoulos

Students who struggle to learn to read face poor outcomes later in life, such as dropping out of high school, becoming teenage parents, or entering the juvenile justice system (Connor, Alberto, Compton, & O'Connor, 2014). Alarming statistics indicate that 19 percent of students with learning disabilities (LD) drop out of school and 12 percent receive a certificate of completion rather than a diploma. One in every two students with a learning disability frequently receives disciplinary action, and one-third of students with learning disabilities have been retained at least once during their schooling (National Center for Learning Disabilities, 2014). Such undesirable outcomes argue for employing only the very best instructional methods.

The achievement gap begins within the first three years of life. By thirty-six months, children living in households of professional caregivers have acquired more than double the vocabulary than children living in poverty (Figurelli, 2015). Early intervention services are the best opportunity to intervene (Dougherty, 2013). Implementing reading interventions early, prior to the fourth grade, promises the best results in closing that achievement gap in reading development.

From birth through grade 3, children are learning the foundational skills needed to read.

After third grade, students are then reading to learn and not learning to read anymore (Figurelli, 2015; Wanzek & Kent, 2012). There are a variety of reading methods considered "best practices," which can seem overwhelming, if not confusing, to teachers and parents. Teachers must be able to support the development of each requisite reading skill in order to develop efficient readers (Dougherty, 2013; Hougen, 2015).

Understanding the concept referred to as "the Matthew effect" and how to prevent and reverse the consequences of this premise is critical for identifying the important components of teaching reading development effectively, especially for students with LD. Through the implementation of evidence-based instructional strategies shown effective for developing efficient readers, this can be accomplished. Teaching strategies that include both explicit instruction, guided practice, and independent practice provide a beneficial combination of support for students with LD as well as struggling readers.

THE MATTHEW EFFECT: WHAT IS IT AND HOW TO REVERSE IT

The Matthew Effect

Perhaps the most widely cited explanation for the poor outcomes associated with reading problems is "the Matthew effect" (Stanovich, 1986). As previously defined, the Matthew effect refers to the ways in which children acquire the skills to learn to read. Research has proven that children who experience early success in reading continue to demonstrate success as they grow and move through the upper grades and into adulthood. Children who struggle or face failures learning to read early on tend to continue to struggle and as a result fall progressively behind academically (Stanovich, 1986; Figurelli, 2015).

Reversing the Matthew Effect

Reversing the Matthew effect among students with learning disabilities means that educators should employ instructional strategies that promote independent reading practice. Both theory (Stanovich, 1986; Stanovich, West, Cunningham, & Cipielewski, 1996) and empirical evidence (Frijters, Barron, & Brunello, 2000; Stanovich & Cunningham, 1993) point to the importance of reading practice. Children who read independently are almost always better readers than those who do not.

Teachers should employ instructional methods that promote both reading skills as well as motivation to read independently. If teachers limit themselves to offering only skills instruction to students with LD, they risk presenting reading as something mandatory and unappealing. Alternatively, if teachers help students with LD view learning to read as a fun and enjoyable activity, they should increase the frequency that these students choose to practice reading independently.

Of critical importance, students with LD experience great difficulty with receptive and expressive language, which in turn affects the processing of language, decoding words, fluency, and ultimately comprehension. These characteristics of LD put a damper on a student's motivation to read (Mele-koglu, 2011).

Research strongly indicates that students with LD require more explicit teacher instruction and opportunities for guided practice before demonstrating success during independent practice (Alves, Kennedy, Brown, & Solis, 2015). Students with LD most likely will require continuous interventions related to reading development. However, educators must consider whether it is developmentally appropriate to engage in interventions meant for K–3 students as LD students attend the upper elementary grades as well as secondary settings.

DEVELOPING EFFICIENT READERS

To become effective readers, children need to master certain skills. These skills build upon one another to enable children to efficiently utilize these abilities to read. Such skills include the structure of language, listening skills, phonological awareness, phonemic awareness, and the alphabetic principle (Hasbrouck & Hougen, 2014). Hasbrouck & Hougen (2014) identifies essential components of reading instruction: word recognition, fluency, vocabulary, and text comprehension.

Word Recognition

Word recognition is the ability to effectively decode words. Students should be taught explicitly how to decode words; this should include explanation of the strategy, teacher modeling of the strategy, and opportunities for guided practice, as well as independent practice. Ehri (2014) offers three strategies that students can apply while reading: decoding, analogizing, and predicting. Students with LD may require small-group, intensive, and explicit strategy instruction in order to learn how to decode multisyllabic words. The intensive instruction should include teacher modeling, guided practice with scaffolding, and opportunities for independent practice (Hasbrouck & Hougen, 2014).

Fluency

Fluency is the ability to read with speed and accuracy. Fluency is directly linked to reading comprehension. When students can efficiently decode words, they are able to increase their fluency. In return, students are then able to devote cognitive energy to other tasks such as comprehending what they are reading (Hasbrouck & Hougen, 2014; Rasinski, Reutzel, Chard, & Linan-Thompson, 2011). One way to increase fluency is to encourage students to read frequently and to read as many types of texts as possible (Hougen, 2015).

Vocabulary

Vocabulary refers to the meaning of words, which plays a large role in reading comprehension. Students with disabilities tend to have less vocabulary knowledge because they are less likely to read as frequently and therefore are exposed to fewer complex vocabulary words (Hasbrouck & Hougen, 2014). There are many opportunities to increase vocabulary development for students, such as through the use of graphic organizers and exposure to challenging texts along with teacher modeling and support.

Text Comprehension

Text comprehension pertains to the understanding of what one has read. For students to become successful in reading comprehension, they must master the previously mentioned components and skills as well as learn strategies to assist with comprehension. There are many strategies that support the development of reading comprehension, before, during, and after reading a text. Strategies such as activating prior knowledge, previewing the text, self-monitoring techniques, the use of graphic organizers, and summarizing are just a few (Solis, Miciak, Vaughn, & Fletcher, 2014).

PEER-ASSISTED LEARNING STRATEGIES

Peer-assisted learning strategies, referred to as PALS, is an attempt to combine reading instruction with activities proven to promote the motivation of students with LD. PALS provides students with LD structured opportunities to read controlled text while engaging with a partner who offers immediate corrective feedback. The structure of PALS helps motivate readers because peers work together to complete common and valued tasks. PALS allows for more cooperative learning opportunities and social interactions to take place. PALS is known to promote the social acceptance of students with LD within inclusion settings (Fuchs & Fuchs, 2005).

What's in a PALS Lesson?

During a typical primary-level PALS lesson, students work together in pairs. To form pairs, students are ranked in the classroom using a rapid automatic naming (RAN) test. RAN is a strong predictor of reading performance (Christo & Davis, 2008). After testing each student in the classroom, students are ranked based on their RAN scores. The teacher then splits the class in half. The highest-scoring student in the top half is placed with the highest-scoring student in the bottom half of the class. The next-to-highest-scoring student in the top half is placed with the next-to-highest-scoring student in the lower half, and so on.

The more accomplished student in each pair is assigned the role of coach. The less accomplished student is assigned the role of reader. The coach's job is to monitor the reader and provide corrective feedback when necessary. The reader's job is to read and cooperate with the coach. Both students take turns being coach and reader throughout each PALS lesson. The higher-achieving student in each pair is always the coach first so that he or she may model each part of the lesson. Best practice dictates that partners rotate every four weeks.

Each PALS lesson has three parts: teacher-directed instruction, sounds and words, and partner reading. Each lesson lasts about forty minutes. Teachers train students in PALS over eight lessons; the training lasts for about two weeks. Teachers are provided with scripted lessons for the training. During training, the students practice as both the coach and the reader. All students learn the correction and modeling procedures. After this training, PALS is implemented three days a week.

PALS Grades 2 through 6

Unlike the PALS program for early elementary students, which focuses on developing the foundational reading skills of beginner reading, the PALS program for grades 2 through 6 supports the development of reading fluency and reading comprehension. Reading comprehension is a critical milestone during these grade levels.

Students with LD find it extremely difficult to learn new skills without having fully mastered the foundational skills needed to move on. It is during this educational period when motivation drops and the achievement gap widens. To develop, maintain, and progress in the areas of fluency and comprehension, PALS activities at the second- through sixth-grade level include such activities as partner reading, retelling, paragraph shrinking, and prediction relay (Institute of Education Sciences, 2012).

Using PALS to Assist English Language Learners with LD

There are two critical areas of language acquisition that English language learners must become proficient in: basic interpersonal communication skills (BICS) and cognitive academic language proficiency (CALP). BICS refers to the language individuals use in social situations. It is the day-to-day language that enables successful social interactions. CALP, on the other hand, refers to formal academic learning, which encompasses speaking, listening, reading, and writing. Some of the higher-order skills necessary to become proficient in CALP include inferencing, synthesizing, comparing, and categorizing (Cummins, 1999; Haynes, n.d.).

There are several pedagogical reasons for incorporating PALS into reading instruction for students with learning disabilities and who are English language learners (ELLs):

1. Students engaged in PALS spend much more time practicing language skills because they are reading aloud.
2. Students are required to summarize and make predictions, which develops higher-order thinking skills.
3. Students are paired up strategically based upon their various ability levels. This allows for individualized and differentiated learning opportunities.
4. Students receive immediate feedback from their peers, which allows for opportunities to recognize mistakes and make corrections, ultimately leading to personal and academic growth. PALS is centered around collaborative learning and reinforcement; thus, student motivation increases (Institute of Education Sciences, 2012).

The use of PALS promotes active participation. Students are required to be involved rather than passively listening to the teacher, which many students with LD and ELL students with LD exhibit. Students spend time observing their peers using various reading strategies. Active peer engagement requires students to read and participate in peer-to-peer discourse through modeling, feedback, and reinforcement (Saenz et al., 2005).

Incorporating PALS into reading instruction provides critical exposure to the skills and practice necessary for students with LD and ELL students with LD to succeed. In support of using PALS, a 2005 study, Saenz et al., examined the effects of implementing PALS in grades 3 through 6 to ELL students with and without LD. The results of the study indicated significant improvement in reading comprehension by both the ELL students with LD and the ELLs without LD.

EVIDENCE-BASED INSTRUCTIONAL STRATEGIES FOR DEVELOPING EFFICIENT READERS

Story Grammar Strategies Guiding Comprehension Development

One well-researched model used to increase reading fluency as well as reading comprehension for students with LD is referred to as story grammar. Research has shown the effectiveness of story grammar at the elementary level all the way through the secondary level. Story grammar essentially refers to story mapping using graphic organizers. When students are using story grammar strategies, they utilize graphic organizers to identify the various elements within a narrative. Story elements refer to such things as characters, setting, the problem, and so forth.

Story grammar strategies involve three critical phases. The first, modeling, involves the teacher explicitly teaching the strategy. It is important that the teacher discuss the different narrative elements, and model how to identify elements within a narrative and how to transfer those elements onto the story map. The second phase, guided practice, allows the students to practice what they learned while having support from the teacher and their peers. The final phase, independent practice, engages the students in individual practice from start to finish (Alves et al., 2015, Wanzek & Kent, 2012).

In a recent study by Alves et al. (2015), two groups of third- and fifth-grade students were provided with story grammar interventions. Most of the students in the study were identified as having LD specifically affecting reading comprehension, while other students were identified as having other types of disabilities, such as ADHD or an emotional disorder. The study examined the effects of an eight-week story grammar intervention. The students participated in four 30-minute modeling sessions, four 30-minute guided practice sessions, and two 30-minute independent practice sessions. After the eight-week intervention, the students' comprehension level was measured again and all students remained above their baseline data (Alves et al., 2015).

INTERVENTIONS TARGETED FOR UPPER ELEMENTARY STUDENTS WITH LD

Wanzek and Kent (2012) examined many studies conducted on the effectiveness of certain types of reading interventions for upper elementary students with LD. The authors closely examined four types of interventions.

1. Word recognition interventions: focused on phonics, word recognition, decoding skills, self-monitoring and self-correcting techniques, and involved both reading and writing activities. All the word recognition studies showed positive outcomes for students with LD.
2. Fluency interventions: refers to repeated readings of a same passage or narrative. The studies involved in the review either conducted their fluency interventions utilizing peer-mediated groups or one-on-one teacher instruction. The results of the studies indicated encouraging results in both decoding and fluency but appeared to show mixed results on the comprehension piece.

3. Comprehension interventions: placed emphasis on development of self-monitoring skills using reading strategies for summarizing, predicting, and questioning. The comprehension intervention studies again had positive outcomes; however, outcomes proved higher for students who mapped while reading.
4. Intervention strategy: story mapping and self-questioning, also yielded beneficial results for students with LD.

CONCLUSION

Evidence has proven that students who struggle to read face poor outcomes later in life (Connor et al., 2014). To address this, teachers must arm themselves with the knowledge and skills necessary to provide evidence-based reading strategies to their students, especially at a young age, since the achievement gap begins within the first three years of life (Dougherty, 2013; Figurelli, 2015).

Students must develop the necessary foundational skills in order to become successful readers. Skills such as understanding the structure of language, phonological awareness, and phonemic awareness, as well as grasping the alphabetic principle are all crucial for developing effective readers. The instructional components that comprise reading development include word recognition and word study, fluency, vocabulary development, and text comprehension (Hasbrouck & Hougen, 2014).

Through peer-assisted learning strategies (PALS) and other reading interventions, the benefit of skills instruction and activities that keep learning to read fun and rewarding are coupled together to provide the most benefit. PALS provides skill instruction through structured opportunities to practice decoding and reading controlled text while allowing students to interact with a partner, offering immediate corrective feedback.

Students receive consistent praise from their partners and reading-related prizes for completing the activities and compete with others and themselves in an appropriate manner to promote success. By coupling skills practice with activities designed to promote greater reading motivation, this should help reverse the Matthew effect (Fuchs & Fuchs, 2005). By increasing reading practice early on, the hope is to increase the long-term success of students with LD (Institute of Education Sciences, 2012).

The other reading interventions presented offer many promising benefits as well. Story grammar instruction, along with the other reading comprehension interventions for older elementary students with learning disabilities, showed hopeful results. One critical component of the interventions geared toward upper elementary students is the teaching of self-monitoring and self-questioning skills (Hougen, 2015; Solis et al., 2014; Wanzek & Kent, 2012).

These skills play an important part in reading, but also in many other content areas, as well as in daily life.

POINTS TO REMEMBER

- Implementing reading interventions early holds the best promise to close the achievement gap for struggling readers.
- Skills instruction as a stand-alone strategy is insufficient to reverse the implications of reading deficits. Combining skills instruction with cooperative learning activities that increase reading practice have proven effective.
- PALS incorporates reading instruction with peer-to-peer activities that, in turn, increases student motivation. Student motivation to read is essential.
- PALS is beneficial for students with learning disabilities and English language learners with learning disabilities, as well as low, average, and high achievers.
- Teaching students to self-monitor and self-question are critical components to any reading intervention program.

REFERENCES

Alves, K., Kennedy, M., Brown, T., & Solis, M. (2015). Story grammar instruction with third and fifth grade students with learning disabilities and other struggling readers. *Learning Disabilities: A Contemporary Journal, 13*(1), 73–93.

Christo, C., & Davis, J. (2008). Rapid naming and phonological processing as predictors of reading and spelling. *California School Psychologist, 13*, 7–18.

Connor, C. M., Alberto, P. A., Compton, D. L., O'Connor, R. E. (2014). *Improving reading outcomes for students with or at risk for reading disabilities: A synthesis of the contributions from the Institute of Education Sciences Research Centers* (NCSER 20143000). Washington, DC: National Center for Special Education Research, Institute of Education Sciences, U.S. Department of Education.

Cummins, J. (1999). *BICS and CALP: Clarifying the distinction.* Opinion Paper. ERIC ED438551.

Dougherty, C. (2013). College and career readiness: The importance of early learning. Policy Report. ACT Research and Policy Organization. Retrieved from http://www.act.org/content/dam/act/unsecured/documents/ImportanceofEarlyLearning.pdf

Ehri, L. C. (2014). Orthographic mapping in the acquisition of reading, spelling memory, and vocabulary learning. *Scientific Studies of Reading, 18*, 5–12.

Figurelli, S. (2015). The Matthew effect [Blog post]. Retrieved from http://inservice.ascd.org/the-matthew-effect/

Frijters, J. C., Barron, R. W., & Brunello, M. (2000). Direct and mediated influences of home literacy and literacy interest on prereaders' oral vocabulary and early written language skill. *Journal of Educational Psychology, 92*, 466–477.

Fuchs, D., & Fuchs, L. (2005). Peer-assisted learning strategies: Promoting word recognition, fluency, and reading comprehension in young children. *Journal of Special Education, 39*(1), 34–44.

Hasbrouck, J., & Hougen, M. (2014). Fluency development for the older student. In M. Hougen (Ed.), *The fundamentals of literacy instruction and assessment* (pp. 6–12). Baltimore, MD: Brookes.

Haynes, J. (n.d.). *Explaining BICS and CALP.* Everything ESL. Retrieved from http://www.everythingesl.net/inservices/bics_calp.php

Hougen, M. (2015). *Evidence-based reading instruction for adolescents grades 6–12. (Document no. IC-13).* Retrieved from University of Florida, Collaboration for Effective Educator, Development, Accountability, and Reform Center website: http://ceedar.education.ufl.edu/tools/innovation-configurations/

Institute of Education Sciences. (2012). Peer-assisted learning strategies. *What Works Clearinghouse.* Retrieved from https://ies.ed.gov/ncee/wwc/Docs/InterventionReports/wwc_pals_013112.pdf

Melekoglu, M. (2011). Impact of motivation to read on reading gains for struggling readers with and without learning disabilities. *Learning Disability Quarterly, 34*(4).

National Center for Learning Disabilities. (2014). *The state of learning disabilities* (3rd ed.). Retrieved from https://www.ncld.org/wp-content/uploads/2014/11/2014-State-of-LD.pdf

Rasinski, T. V., Reutzel, D. R., Chard, D., & Linan-Thompson, S. (2011). Reading fluency. In M. L. Kamil, P. D. Pearson, B. Moje, & P. Afflerbach (Eds.), *Handbook of reading research* (Vol. 4, pp. 286–319). New York, NY: Routledge.

Solis, M., Miciak, J., Vaughn, S., & Fletcher, J. (2014). Why intensive interventions matter: Longitudinal studies of adolescents with reading disabilities and poor reading comprehension. *Learning Disability Quarterly, 37*(4), 218–229.

Stanovich, K. E. (1986). Matthew effects in reading: Some consequences of individual differences in the acquisition of literacy. *Reading Research Quarterly, 21*, 360–407.

Stanovich, K. E., & Cunningham, A. E. (1993). Where does knowledge come from? Specific associations between print exposure and information acquisition. *Journal of Educational Psychology, 85*, 211–229.

Stanovich, K. E., West, R. F., Cunningham, A. E., & Cipielewski, J. (1996). The role of inadequate print exposure as a determinant of reading comprehension problems. In C. Cornoldi & J. Oakhill (Eds.), *Reading comprehension difficulties: Processes and interventions* (pp. 15–32). Mahwah, NJ: Erlbaum.

Wanzek, J., & Kent, S. (2012). Reading interventions for students with learning disabilities in the upper elementary grades. *Learning Disabilities: A Contemporary Journal, 10*(1), 5–16.

Chapter Seven

Teaching Collaborative Strategic Reading (CSR) to Students with Learning Disabilities

Alison Boardman, Sharon Vaughn, and Janette Klingner

Jason Rivera said, "I have a clunk. I don't know what the word 'carriage' means." Juan Sanchez replied, "Who can help with the clunk 'carriage'? Ok, no. Well, then read the sentence before 'carriage,' the sentence with the word 'carriage' in it, and the sentence after the one with 'carriage' in it, and see if you can figure it out." Both Jason and Juan are students in Melanie Ross's fifth-grade class. They learned how to use the "clunk" strategy, as well as several other reading strategies, as part of an instructional approach called collaborative strategic reading, or CSR.

WHAT IS COLLABORATIVE STRATEGIC READING (CSR)?

Collaborative strategic reading (CSR) takes advantage of the growing knowledge base indicating that students benefit when taught specific strategies to enhance their understanding of text but should not be overwhelmed with so many strategies that they are unable to decide which ones to use (Duke, Pearson, Strachan, & Billman, 2011; Kendeou, van de Broek, Helder, & Karlsson, 2014; Klingner, Vaughn, Boardman, & Swanson, 2012). Pikulski (1998) argues that sound pedagogy in reading comprehension instruction would call for teaching four or five strategies.

CSR teaches students four critical reading comprehension strategies along with specific procedures for how to apply them independently. To enhance implementation of the strategies and to ensure each student has maximum opportunities for practice, CSR is implemented in small groups (usually four students), with each student in the group assuming a critical role (e.g., leader, clunk expert, gist expert, question expert). CSR also works well with student pairs.

WHAT RESEARCH SUPPORTS CSR?

CSR was designed to capitalize on effective practices to enhance the understanding of and learning from text. These strategies combined with collaborative grouping structures and peer pairing have yielded effective outcomes for students from elementary through middle school. Below is a summary of CSR studies conducted with low-achieving students and students with LD in fourth through eighth grade. An asterisk (*) indicates that the results are statistically significant.

Klingner, Vaughn, and Schumm (1998)

In this quasi-experimental study, 85 fourth-grade students in large, culturally and linguistically diverse inclusive classrooms were randomly assigned to receive CSR or to continue receiving their teachers' typical instructional practices (ES = .44 for total sample*).

Klingner, Vaughn, Argüelles, Hughes, and Ahwee (2004)

In this quasi-experimental study, 306 fourth-grade students in large, culturally and linguistically diverse inclusive classrooms were randomly assigned to receive CSR or to continue receiving their teachers' typical instructional practices (ES = .19 for total sample*; .25 for high/average-achieving students; .51 for low-achieving students; .38 for students with LD).

Vaughn et al. (2011)

This randomized control trial included 866 seventh- and eighth-grade students in language arts and reading classes with a focus on struggling readers. Teachers taught some sections with CSR and some sections using typical instruction (ES= .12 for total sample*; .36 for low-achieving students).

Kim et al. (2006)

In this quasi-experimental study, 34 sixth- through eighth-grade students with LD in diverse reading and language arts classrooms were assigned to receive CSR or continue with typical instruction. Teachers taught in both conditions (ES = .50 for students with LD*).

Boardman, Klingner, Buckley, Annamma, and Lasser (2015)

In another randomized control trial 1,074 sixth- through eighth-grade students in diverse science and social studies classrooms were assigned to CSR or typical instruction. Teachers taught in both conditions. This study focused on ELLs and struggling readers (ES = .18 for total sample*).

Boardman et al. (2016)

In this randomized control trial, 1,372 fourth- and fifth-grade students were assigned by classroom to receive CSR or typical instruction. This study focused on students with LD (ES = .52 for students with LD*).

WHAT ARE THE FOUR STRATEGIES TAUGHT IN CSR?

The four strategies taught in CSR are: preview, click and clunk, get the gist, and wrap up. Go to www.toolkit.csrcolorado.org/ to download the teacher and student materials described in this chapter and to watch examples of CSR in action.

Preview

This step occurs before reading. During the preview strategy, students preview the text by reading the titles and subtitles, looking at images and captions, and making connections to what they already know about the topic. The primary goals of previewing are that students (a) generate interest about the text they will read, (b) stimulate their background knowledge and associations with the text, and (c) are provided with relevant information and the purpose for reading.

The teacher first introduces the topic of the reading and provides students with a brainstorm question. For example, in a reading on earth-friendly fabrics, a brainstorm question might be, "What do you already know about activities that are helpful to the earth?" Students take one to two minutes to answer the brainstorm question and share their responses with a partner or their small group. The teacher then presents a few key vocabulary terms to build background knowledge (e.g., sustainable development, biodiversity, fabric), using images, a short video, or demonstrations to provide examples.

The teacher then sets the purpose for reading. For instance, in the earth-friendly fabrics reading, the teacher might say, "Today we are going to read about how fabrics, or clothes, can be made in ways that are not harmful to the earth." The preview is short, usually five to ten minutes. Previewing is a skill that can be used throughout the day and across the curriculum. It does not need to be used only when students are implementing CSR, but can be used to preview the day, current events, or a new topic the teacher is presenting prior to actual instruction.

Learning logs are written records that provide students with a tool for recording what they are learning and a means for teachers to monitor the progress of individual students, pairs, or groups. The learning log can be adapted to support individuals or groups of learners. A few examples include providing word banks, strategy cues that provide the steps of a strategy, sentence frames, or adjusting the amount of writing space or the layout.

Click and Clunk

This skill occurs during reading. While previewing is a skill that is used prior to reading, click and clunk is a self-monitoring strategy that is implemented during reading. When students "click," they recognize material that they know a lot about, and it makes sense to them. They are ready to extend the information provided in the text and think about it in new ways. When students "clunk," they identify words or concepts that they don't understand and need to know more about in order to make sense of what they are reading and learning. Students are taught to click and clunk while they read by writing down words that they don't understand or cannot describe.

Once students have read a designated amount of text, they discuss their clicks and clunks. The greater emphasis in the groups is on solving clunks. Students are taught clunk strategies, and the clunk expert in the group guides students through the strategies in an attempt to "de-clunk" words or ideas that they do not know. Clunk strategies are referred to as "fix-up" strategies as they help students repair meaning that is lost until they understand the clunk. Once students have identified the meaning of a clunk, they put the definition back in the text to be sure it makes sense and then record the definition in their learning logs.

In Tami Taylor's class, students in one of the groups were stumped by the word "noxious." At first Antonio suggested that it means "when you are sick and feel like you are going to throw up." Lucy, the clunk expert, said, "No . . . that's nauseous." She reminded the group to reread the sentence (fix-up strategy #1). She read, "Noxious chemicals are used to kill bugs and weeds." After a brief discussion, the group determined that based on the context, noxious means bad or toxic. Edward tried their definition in the sentence and the students recorded their new understanding in their learning logs.

CSR Fix-Up Strategies

- Reread the sentence with the clunk and look for key ideas to help you figure out the word. Think about what makes sense.

- Reread the sentences before and after the clunk, looking for clues.
- Break the word apart and look for word parts (prefixes, suffixes, root words) or smaller words you know.
- Does the clunk have a cognate that makes sense?

Get the Gist

This step also occurs during reading. Like click and clunk, "get the gist" is practiced during reading. The purpose of this strategy is to teach students to identify the most critical information about what they have just read, or, in other words, to identify the main idea. The main idea is an important reading comprehension skill.

While many teachers ask students to tell them the main idea, few teachers teach youngsters how to identify the main idea. With get the gist, students are taught to identify the most important point in the text by rephrasing the key idea in their own words—limiting their response to about ten words (Fuchs, Fuchs, Mathes, & Simmons, 1997). The intent is to teach students to synthesize a short section of text by learning to convey only the key information and to exclude unnecessary details.

Jane Headows teaches her students to get the gist by focusing on a two-paragraph section of text at a time. She asks them to read the text, and while they are reading, to think about identifying the most important "who" or "what." After the students read, she asks them to tell her the most important who or what and the most important ideas about the who or what (Fuchs et al., 1997). She calls on several students and then continually refers back to the class to get their feedback about what aspects of the gist were helpful. She then asks each student to write his or her own gist.

In CSR, students learn each strategy one at a time, and then apply all the strategies in small student-led groups. Learning the skill individually first facilitates students' success as they work in their groups. The learning log is one way for students to record their gists as they read.

Wrap Up

"Wrap up" is like "preview" in that it occurs only once during the process, this time after students have read the entire text. Students are taught to wrap up by generating the kinds of questions that a teacher would ask about what they have read. The purpose of wrap up is to teach students to identify the most significant ideas about the entire passage they've read and to assist them with understanding and remembering what they've learned.

While students practice the gist after reading short sections of text (a couple of paragraphs to about a page, depending on text complexity), they wrap up only at the end of the material they have covered for the entire lesson, usually one to three pages of text.

Tiffany Royal, a fifth-grade teacher, provides the following question stems to her students to assist them in doing a wrap-up (adapted from Rosenshine & Meister, 1992):

- How were they the same? Different?
- What do you think would happen if _____?
- What do you think caused _____ to happen?
- How would you compare and contrast _____?
- What might have prevented the problem from happening?
- What is the strength and weakness of _____?
- How would you interpret _____?

One of the ways Sylvia Gleason taught her students to wrap up was by providing each group with four index card–sized pieces of paper. She asked each group to formulate a question on one side of the index card and the answer on the back. Students then shared their questions with other groups. Sylvia also taught her students to ask three types of questions:

- Easy: the answer can be found right in the text and answered in one or two words. For example, "What was the cowboy carrying on the horse? The mail."
- Harder: the answer is in the text, but it requires putting information together to make the answer, usually in one or more sentences. For example, "How did Joey know he was late for the party? He saw lots of people in the yard, and he noticed that the food on the plates had already been eaten."
- Hardest: the answer is partly in the text and partly in the student's head and requires inferences or connections outside of the text. For example, "Why did Maggie give up sailing?"

After students ask and answer each other's questions, they write a short review statement, usually one to two sentences long, that includes the most important information from the entire passage. Students share their review statements, providing evidence from the text to justify their responses. Finally, the teacher brings the entire class back together to do a brief whole-group wrap-up. At this time the teacher might choose to make connections to the topic of study or to an essential question.

The teacher might also choose to review a difficult clunk or to return to the preview to see how students have added to what they knew about the topic at the start of the lesson. For instance, in an eighth-grade science class, during the whole-class wrap-up, Nettie Welk asked her students how the techniques used to clean up an oil spill in the Gulf of Mexico in the article they read using CSR related to what they were learning about the separation of liquids and solids in their chemistry unit.

In CSR, the teacher bookends the lesson, beginning by setting the purpose and ending by revisiting the purpose and helping students make curricular and real-world connections. In between, students take ownership of the process as they read, apply strategies, and negotiate meaning in their collaborative groups.

HOW DOES THE TEACHER ORGANIZE GROUPS OR PAIRS TO TEACH CSR?

How do students work in their collaborative groups with their defined roles? Roles are a significant aspect of CSR because students work most effectively when they have designated responsibilities and when there is enough interdependence among group members that cooperation is essential to group effectiveness (Johnson & Johnson, 1984). Typically, the teacher organizes students into heterogeneous groups of four, and assigns each student an expert role (e.g., leader, clunk expert, gist expert, question expert).

Students may rotate roles regularly so that everyone in the group has the opportunity to experience and learn from taking on different roles. CSR has also been used effectively with student pairs. Students work together to read the text, apply the strategies, and complete the learning log. The roles in the group are:

- Leader: This student serves as the group guide and is responsible for ensuring the involvement of all group members. The leader tells students when to read, nudges members to participate, serves as a timekeeper, and contacts the teacher when needed.
- Clunk expert: This student guides the group in following the steps to figure out a difficult word or concept.
- Gist expert: This student guides the group toward the development of their individual gists and helps determine that gists are the right length and contain the key ideas. The gist expert also leads a discussion in which students share and provide feedback on their gist statements.
- Question expert: The question expert facilitates the question generation process, being sure that students are writing different kinds of questions, using resources such as question stems, and asking and answering each other's questions.

WHAT ROLE DOES THE TEACHER PLAY DURING CSR?

Introducing the CSR Strategies

Teachers first introduce each CSR strategy, one at a time, by modeling and thinking aloud. They also provide many opportunities for students to practice individually, with partners, and in small groups. As students learn the strategies, they can begin to incorporate the expert roles to develop the discussion component.

Text Selection and Lesson Planning

CSR teachers need to locate and prepare materials. There are certain types of reading materials with which CSR works best. CSR was designed to be used with expository text found in social studies and other content-area textbooks and curricula. Texts with well-formed, interesting passages that include definitions of key vocabulary terms in context provide the best opportunities for implementation of this teaching tool. Many teachers also use CSR with *Weekly Reader*, *Junior Scholastic*, or a similar nonfiction publication that is relevant and meaningful. Whenever possible it is best to select texts that align with curriculum.

CSR teachers divide the text into two to three short sections (usually a few paragraphs each). They also identify the brainstorm question and key vocabulary terms to preteach as well as possible clunks that students might identify as they are reading. The teacher writes possible gists for each section, questions, and a review statement. Doing this brief preparation allows teachers to maximize the quality and specificity of feedback they provide to students because they can compare their own responses with those generated by students.

Facilitating Group Work

Once students have learned how to apply the CSR strategies in their cooperative learning groups, the teacher's role is to circulate among groups and provide ongoing assistance. Joyce Duryea values the opportunity CSR affords her to listen in on students' conversations and hear "learning as it happens." She continuously monitors individual and group progress. Sometimes when students are struggling to understand a difficult clunk, she listens without interrupting but makes a note to bring up the clunk later with the whole class.

At other times, she models how to figure out the word (or get the gist, as the case may be). There are also occasions when she merely drops a hint or gives a clue, enabling students who were "stuck" to continue on their own. She provides positive feedback to students and encourages reticent students to participate. It is to be expected that students will need assistance learning to work in cooperative groups, implementing the strategies, and mastering academic content.

There are five important tasks the teacher can fulfill during CSR group work (Klingner et al., 2001):

1. Spend extended time with each group at least once every two weeks.
2. Monitor the performance of each group.
3. Monitor the performance of each student within the group.
4. Highlight the performance of students or groups who are implementing the strategies exceedingly well.
5. Take a note on common clunks or difficult gists and teach to the class as a whole.

CSR teachers use a variety of follow-up activities to reinforce the key vocabulary and important concepts students have learned from reading a day's lesson. Each group might complete a different follow-up activity (e.g., a semantic map, mnemonic devices, a Venn diagram) to share with other groups. Students can also prepare games and activities as homework.

CONCLUSION

CSR is an excellent tool for enhancing comprehension and content learning, but it is not intended to be the only form of content-area instruction a teacher uses. It should replace whole-class read-the-chapter-and-answer-the-questions types of lessons, but should not replace other activities associated with effective content-area instruction such as hands-on projects, experiments, or inquiry-based learning.

Educators greatly value the benefits their students receive from using CSR. Tiffany Royal, an expert CSR implementer, stated, "What I like best is that my students learn how to understand what they read while they improve their vocabulary. Also it helps on our end of the year [state assessments]." Sallie Gotch, a special education teacher, added, "CSR is great for kids with LD because they contribute to their groups and feel successful, and they get the help they need with their reading." Referring to her students identified as limited English proficient, Lucille Sullivan noted, "I can't believe how well they did, how much they learned. I've seen so much improvement in their English. And they are participating more in other subjects, too. They seem more confident."

POINTS TO REMEMBER

- In CSR, students use talk and strategies as tools to support meaning construction before, during, and reading.
- Students need explicit instruction in reading strategies along with weekly opportunities to practice them in content-focused text.
- Teachers choose important text that is integrated into curricula and aligns with learning objectives.
- CSR resources such as learning logs and expert role cards facilitate the CSR process and help students take ownership for reading and understanding.
- Collaborative group work is facilitated by the teacher, who assigns students to heterogeneous groups, monitors group and individual understanding, and provides assistance as needed.
- The teacher's role is key to the success of CSR. Setting a purpose for reading and building background knowledge with a few key vocabulary words as well as bringing the class back together to solidify big ideas at the end of the lesson helps students remember and relate the text content to other ideas they are learning.

REFERENCES

Boardman, A. G., Klingner, J. K., Buckley, P., Annamma, S., & Lasser, C. J. (2015). The efficacy of collaborative strategic reading in middle school science and social studies classes. *Reading & Writing: An Interdisciplinary Journal, 28*(9), 1257–1283.

Boardman, A. G., Vaughn, S., Buckley, P., Reutebuch, C. K., Roberts, G., & Klingner, J. K. (2016). Collaborative strategic reading for students with learning disabilities in upper elementary classrooms. *Exceptional Children, 82*(4), 409–427.

Duke, N., Pearson, D., Strachan, S., & Billman, A. (2011). Essential elements of fostering and teaching reading comprehension. In S. J. Samuels & A. E. Farstrup (Eds.), *What research has to say about reading instruction* (4th ed., pp. 51–93). Newark, DE: International Reading Association.

Fuchs, D., Fuchs, L. S., Mathes, P. G., & Simmons, D. C. (1997). Peer-assisted learning strategies: Making classrooms more responsive to diversity. *American Educational Research Journal, 34*(1), 174–206.

Johnson, D. W., & Johnson, R. T. (1984). *Cooperation in the classroom.* Minneapolis, MN: Interaction Book Co.

Kendeou, P., van den Broek, P., Helder, A., & Karlsson, J. (2014). A cognitive view of reading comprehension: Implications for reading difficulties. *Learning Disabilities Research & Practice, 29*(1), 10–16.

Kim, A., Vaughn, S., Klingner, J. K., Woodruff, A. L., Reutebuch, C. K., & Kouzekanani, K. (2006). Improving the reading comprehension of middle school students with disabilities through computer-assisted collaborative strategic reading. *Remedial and Special Education, 27*, 235–249.

Klingner, J. K., Vaughn, S., Boardman, A. G., & Swanson, E. (2012). *Now we get it! Boosting comprehension with collaborative strategic reading.* San Francisco, CA: Jossey-Bass Teacher.

Klingner, J. K., Vaughn, S., Hughes, M. T., Arguelles, M. E., & Ahwee, S. (2001). *Outcomes for students with and without learning disabilities through collaborative strategic reading.* Manuscript in progress.

Klingner, J. K., Vaughn, S., Hughes, M. T., Arguelles, M. E., & Ahwee, S. (2004). Collaborative strategic reading: "Real-world" lessons from classroom teachers. doi.10.1177/07419325040250050301

Pikulski, J. J. (1998). *Improving reading achievement: Major instructional considerations for the primary grades.* Paper presented at the Commissioner's Second Annual Reading Conference, Austin, Texas.

Rosenshine, B., & Meister, C. (1992). The use of scaffolds for teaching higher-level cognitive strategies. *Educational Leadership, 49,* 26–33.

Vaughn, S., Klingner, J. K., Swanson, E., Boardman, A., Roberts, G., Mohammed, S., Stillman-Spisak, S. (2011). Efficacy of collaborative strategic reading with middle school students. *American Educational Research Journal, 48,* 938–954.

Chapter Eight

Beyond the Schoolhouse Door

*Promoting Reading Partnerships in
the Home and Community*

Christine N. Michael and Nicholas D. Young

Creating strong readers is a community commitment that goes well beyond what happens within the classroom. In this day and age, reading is a necessity for all students, and it is particularly important that learners with disabilities join the ranks of the literate. In her book *Reading in the Wild* (2014), author Donalyn Miller quotes the findings of a 2014 National Assessment of Educational Progress (NAEP) report, which compared children across states before Common Core State Standards began:

> Beyond the research and reform efforts in reading instruction, the development of lifelong literacy habits and abilities that are fostered through family and environmental support are of growing concern. More and more, educators and parents agree that students must not only develop the ability to comprehend what they read, but also develop an orientation to literacy that leads to lifelong reading and learning. (p. xix)

Gallagher (2009) bemoans the "killing" of reading in his book *Readicide*. Among the forces killing literacy and lifelong reading in our country, he counts such things as valuing test takers over lifelong readers, requiring students to read texts that are too difficult for them, and not providing deep enough instruction for students to access classic but difficult texts. Additionally, he suggests that students are not allowing enough recreational reading, and that educators layer the reading experience with too many reading journals, sticky notes and other ancillary tactics.

According to Gallagher (2009), there are three keys to developing life-long readers: interesting books, time to read, and a place to read. While his book laments the killing of reading in schools, the same factors can be said to influence literacy outside of the schoolhouse. Author Jon Scieszka, now the country's first ambassador for Young People's Literature, warns of the "death spiral" that can come if children don't read regularly. "It's where kids aren't reading and then are worse at reading because they aren't reading, and then they read less because it is hard and they get worse, and then they see themselves as non-readers" (as cited in Gallagher, 2009, p. 85).

A recent National Endowment for the Arts study found that in 2012, 55 percent of adults over eighteen participated in voluntary reading, that is, not for work or school. Only 18 percent of adults in the United States labeled themselves "frequent" or "avid" readers of literary texts, 24 percent were light readers, and 10 percent were moderate readers. The study goes on to state that "reading is positively correlated with educational level and family income" (National Endowment for the Arts, 2015, p. 71). Slightly different statistics are available from a 2015 Pew Research Study, which recounts that approximately 26 percent of American adults have not "read a book in whole or in part in the past year" and, conversely, that 73 percent read at least one book (quoted in Perrin, 2016, n.p.).

Even the most skilled and committed educators struggle with how to engage families and the larger community in literacy promotion, as all educators must court involvement and reinforcement of literacy beyond their classroom walls if they are to meet their end goals of lifelong literacy for all students. In contemporary society, families and communities are frequently overwhelmed with responsibilities and issues; finding the time for out-of-school reading is not often the top priority, particularly with children and adolescents who struggle with reading; however, when the school can engage families or communities, the impact on student literacy is profound.

Ferlazzo (2009) points out an important key for school-family-community engagement in the literacy process: he defines "engaging parents" as recognizing that family and community members have the potential to be the "leaders" in reading initiatives—or any initiatives, for that matter. To truly engage parents and community, the school must begin by tapping that leadership potential by asking parents (and students) their ideas about literacy development and what might work with their children and their particular community of culture.

This is particularly important when there are subcommunities who may be marginalized in the educational process. These might include minority communities, new immigrants, students with disabilities, or families for whom English is not the primary language of the home. The goal of family literacy movements is to create safe, welcoming, and "doable" programs that invite children, their families, and community partners into a collaboration that leads to a more literate lifetime for all.

WHAT IS A FAMILY LITERACY PROGRAM?

Family literacy programs are approaches to education in which parents and children learn and grow together. Family literacy programs have multiple, mutually supportive goals: addressing the literacy strengths and needs of the family/community while promoting adults' involvement in children's education, recognizing adults as a powerful influence on children's academic success. Since there is a reciprocal nature in parent-child relationships, successful programs include both parent-initiated and child-initiated activities to build and nurture the development of those relationships and to increase both parties' motivation to learn (Family Literacy, 2015).

Family literacy programs integrate both early childhood and adult-focused education in their initiatives. Effective programs provide:

- Interactive literacy activities between parents and their children
- Education for parents in facilitating children's learning and becoming full partners in their education
- Parent literacy training that leads to economic self-sufficiency and meets adults' stated goals
- Age-appropriate education to prepare children for success in school and life experiences (Family Literacy, 2015)

Many highly engaging programs focus solely on children and adolescents' literacy. While the schoolhouse is the obvious first stage for literacy development, home and community are no less critical in the formation of fluent readers. Strong partnerships between all parties set the tone for promoting the importance of lifelong reading. What are the challenges that these partners face, and what strategies, activities, and habits have been proven successful in nurturing reading habits that will last long beyond formal school years?

WHAT WORKS?

Staying Engaged

A 2007 study by the National Endowment for the Arts, the largest such survey of American reading ever conducted, found "calamitous, universal falling off of reading" at about age thirteen. This falling off continues forward throughout students' lives (as cited in Gallagher, 2009, p. 112). The same survey, titled "To Read or Not to Read," mirrored radical changes in the way reading plays out in current students' lives.

These are the first generation of students who were surrounded by electronic media from birth; they read less, and read less well than previous generations. Because they read less, they read less well; because they read less well, they do less well in school and participate less in civic life. The kinds of reading that they do via the Internet tends toward more shallow, headline, blurb and blog type of reading. In the past ten years, the reading proficiency of college graduates fell 23 percent and half of the adults in this country do not read or read to their children, while 55 percent of those who read below a "basic" level are unemployed (Gallagher, 2009).

It is generally agreed that about the time that students enter early adolescence, adults in the home become less involved in literacy activities with them. Beers (2005) found that middle school readers recalled many reading activities within their families, dating back to their earliest memories. Among the literacy activities that they recall were prolonged reading; reading aloud with their parents; parents modeling reading activities; the presence of a "home library"; having books and other reading materials in their cars or at appointments or vacations; and having bedtime stories.

The same study (Beers, 2005) found that the parents of the students interviewed also related these activities. Additionally, the adults said that if they sought child care for their children, they looked for settings in which literacy activities had primacy. When these children entered school, they already saw reading as valuable and pleasurable. Sadly, a recent Scholastic study (Scholastic & YouGov, 2014) found that of the one thousand children surveyed, 40 percent (or four in ten) "say they wished their parents had continued reading aloud to them" (p. 6). While it may be awkward for families to continue the read-aloud tradition with older children, it is essential to make family literacy a priority. Parents should still consider reading aloud with their children until there is active resistance; older children can practice their reading by sharing with younger siblings. Movies, videos, and documentaries serve as springboards for awakening interest in older students, by asking them to compare and contrast the book and movie.

Smith and Wilhelm (2002, 2006) note that there was greater incentive among their research participants to read texts that were "exportable"—that could easily be exported into a conversation. Such exportable texts can be as simple as sports updates, headlines, financial information, movie reviews, or weather stories; they can be derived from print or from digital means, but the point is that if shared in common with another family member or friend (such as a passion for the Red Sox, for example), they can spur interest in reading for informational purposes.

Skillful parents and teachers can then extend the reading experience through suggesting biographies or autobiographies of favorite players, memoirs of a particular season, sports analysis, magazines, or blogs. Having subscriptions (print or online) to magazines of interest is another way to engage readers. Families and community members need to stay the course with middle school and secondary students as far as literacy efforts are concerned. For middle school students, Henderson (2011) proposes the following strategies:

- Help young adolescents find reading that they will like; do not criticize choices, even if they are not parental favorites.
- Motivation is increased by reluctant readers having choice and control over what they read.
- Continue to model reading and read together, even if it is parallel reading, rather than reading the same book aloud.
- Praise even small steps toward progress.
- Give books as gifts and choose books that relate to students' passions, and help middle schoolers see how reading can be linked to their passions in real life.

Family also should engage in adultlike discussions about what their children are reading and use a child's interest in social media to extend his or her reading (Henderson, 2011). Teens who struggle with reading are challenging, in that it is often extremely difficult to get them to sit down to read. Many of the strategies suggested for middle school students still apply, such as choice, modeling reading, meaningful discussion, and praise. It is also important for both groups to find series by the same author or books clustered on a particular topic, so that preknowledge and anticipation can ease reading difficulties (Henderson, 2011).

Understanding the Reading Process

A key to being able to support struggling readers is a firm grasp of the process of reading itself. The more that family members understand the component factors of reading (phonemic awareness, phonics, fluency, vocabulary, and comprehension) and where their child is struggling, the more they can bolster the weaker areas while using his or her competencies. Family should seek out specific information from their children's teachers and be certain to ask questions so that they understand how best to address areas of need at home.

Along with targeting a student's strengths and areas of weakness, family should ask his or her teachers to make sure that assigned work is at the correct developmental level if reading assignments and homework consistently seem too hard. Kittle (2013) believes that the language of what students are reading must be accessible, as "enjoyment is more likely and thus [their] willingness to keep trying. We can and must give students rich experiences with literature, but we also must pay attention to how texts can discourage them" (p. 15).

It is important for family to feel empowered to ask the critical questions necessary to be active helpers in their child's literacy education. For example, in addition to identifying and discussing each child's strengths and interests, teachers should: share the child's profile of reading skills and discuss worries or concerns; have clear strategies to address those concerns; be able to clarify the reading instruction program being used; and discuss collaborative "next steps" to best assist the child in and out of school (PBS.org, 2002).

Seeing the Connection between Reading and Writing

For many years, reading and writing were seen as such separate processes that they were taught independently. Recent research, however, demonstrates that they are far more interdependent than once was believed. To help struggling readers improve, one must also take steps to improve their writing (Graham & Hebert, 2010).

An extensive study conducted by the Carnegie Corporation found that writing is the underutilized tool for improving reading skills and content learning (Graham & Hebert, 2010).

The study promotes three primary strategies to improve literacy through writing: have students write about what they are reading; teach them the skills that go into producing the texts that they are reading; and increase the amount of writing that students do. Family involvement in the writing process augments what happens in schools and cements the relationship between the two processes.

There are multiple, meaningful ways to capitalize on natural needs for writing: thank-you notes for gifts received; requests for products or services; letters to the editor; communications with friends or family members at a distance; keeping a journal. There also are ways of personalizing reading responses, such as keeping reading logs, responding to favorite books, or writing to beloved characters or authors. Students can be helped to write their own books and then read them aloud, or families can pen their family histories. Younger students can dictate their stories to older ones and then share them in reading partnerships. Anything that personalizes the reading/writing experience improves motivation.

In their collection of strategies for bridging out-of-school literacies with classroom practice, Hull and Schultz (2002) highlight some of the innovative activities occurring around the country. For example, in Chicago, young students are involved in an after-school computer club program called the Fifth Dimension project, which links children from diverse U.S. neighborhoods with kids in Russia and targets students at risk for reading and writing failures in school and engages them in computer games designed to advance their learning.

The key writing component involves communications facilitated by "the Wizard," a fantasy figure that the students believe resides in the telecommunications system. Students receive personalized messages from the Wizard, respond, and have written dialogues with diverse peers, mediated by the Wizard. This highly engaging form of writing and responding has been shown to increase motivation to write, length of writing, and reading skills (Hull & Schultz, 2002).

Developing Vocabulary

Vocabulary skills vary widely among students classified with learning disabilities. For some, oral vocabulary is an area of great strength. But for those who struggle with language and reading, actively building a rich vocabulary can ease the reading struggle. When children have delayed language, it may seem natural to tend to talk less to them. While some reduction of language may be helpful, all children need good stimulation and the opportunity to build their vocabulary bank.

Wiener (1988) emphasizes the importance of informal, unstructured conversation to spark children's learning. Although his focus is on normally developing children, all parents should talk while they are doing things with their children to enhance their vocabulary and concepts. When parents externalize their thinking and actions, the dialogue strengthens the child's vocabulary. So does modeling an interest in words, their meanings, and their uses.

Children with vocabulary deficits are especially vulnerable as they become readers in middle school, due to a steep increase in the level of vocabulary used in texts around the fourth grade (Spear-Swerling, 2006).

Parents should discuss their child's vocabulary assessment with classroom teachers and specialists to determine if targeted instruction in vocabulary is warranted, and what strategies can be used at home to complement classroom activities. New technologies, including electronic and online resources, can also prove valuable.

Finding Accommodations and Strategies

There is a host of alternative ways to help readers who wrestle with decoding, reading retention, or comprehension. These alternative approaches are particularly helpful at home; for example, readers with memory problems can be taught memory aids, such as mnemonics; students with comprehension problems can use sticky notes to record seminal information from what they are reading. Techniques for family do not require advanced training;

they can be as simple as reading aloud daily, playing word games such as Scrabble, or using a Kindle to play Words with Friends.

DEAR time (drop everything and read) can be imported to the home, so that parents and others are modeling good reading habits; students can "teach" family members what they learn when they read, or dramatize their selections. Again, forming a strong, positive relationship with a child's teachers and specialists is the key to using the accommodations and strategies most effective with each reader. Family can ask for computer programs or sites that target their child's reading needs; they can also ask for suggestions for enhancing vocabulary, as a rich vocabulary aids in reading success.

Using Multiple Mentoring Models

Struggling readers may benefit greatly from a reading buddy or mentor. The national Read, Think, Share mentoring program takes college student mentors and pairs them with students from low-income backgrounds. Students have a wide range of books to choose from; they discuss the book forum-style and are provided with "positive feedback and academic support, but also time spent corresponding with strong role models" (Reader to Reader, n.d.). While the primary goal is to build core skills in writing and reading, the program also aims to build social skills and connections through mentoring.

Mentors are specifically chosen for their academic achievement, social skills, community involvement, and diversity, as well as their potential to inspire at-risk students. As young adults themselves, the mentors can relate to their mentees in ways that diverge from the way teachers and other adults relate to them. These programs involve older students forming friendships with and mentoring younger children in a structured environment. Cross-age peer programs provide growth and learning opportunities for both mentors and mentees, resulting in gains for both.

Such programs recognize the importance of peer relationships for children and adolescents. Cross-age peer programs take advantage of children's increasing interest in peer friendships as they enter the middle school and secondary school years. But younger children who are reluctant readers also thrive in relationships with "reading buddies" who act as informal mentors.

Mentees' natural tendency to look up to slightly older youth means that they view their mentor as a role model and someone worth listening to. Peer mentors also benefit from interacting with each other in positive ways through the volunteer experience, often building new relationships beyond their normal circle of friends. There are additional benefits beyond reading gains. Peer mentors also can assist with transitions in mentees' lives. As Garringer and MacRae (2008) point out:

> Mentees in elementary or middle school benefit from having

an older student help them through the challenges of moving to a new school and the accompanying changes in social relationships that brings. High school mentors build personal skills and confidence that can help prepare them for their lives after high school. Their involvement in the program can also be a meaningful addition to applications for colleges and future jobs. (p. 1)

Older students, even those who may not be highly proficient readers, can take pride in being "reading buddies" for younger students and students with reading disabilities. In turn, this can boost their interest in becoming a more proficient reader.

Reading mentoring programs can also utilize new technologies. With online connections, rural areas or programs, constrained by the availability of face-to-face mentors, can develop effective programs. As an example, one program accomplished motivating Native American youths while connecting them to college-age mentors three thousand miles away (Reader to Reader, n.d.). Community and business members also can be mentors, either in school or by creating innovative, on-site programs. Tracey, Hornery, Seaton, Craven, and Yeung (2014) found that mentoring school-aged readers had powerful benefits for both the mentors and mentees.

ADDRESSING THE GENDER GAP IN READING

By the middle school grades, a serious gap in reading achievement exists between boys and girls. Jacobson (2014) notes because boys are less verbal than girls, the contemporary, standards-based curricula required now of all schools can leave boys behind academically as early as fourth or fifth grade. One result of this disparity in performance is an image in boys' minds that they are not as proficient in reading as girls are.

According to Jacobson (2014) boys and girls view reading "in fundamentally different ways," with girls wanting to relate to the books' characters and finding reading fiction a pleasure, while boys want to be able to immediately use what they read (p. 48). Boys need to see a rationale for what they are reading, and they need a real-world use for the text. Jacobson (2014) finds that middle school boys most enjoy reading "magazines, graphic novels, and books that feature gory scenes or gross humor" (p. 4).

A seminal work on boys and literacy is Smith and Wilhelm's (2002) *Reading Don't Fix No Chevys: Literacy in the Lives of Young Men*. In the book, the authors explore some of the underlying reasons for boys' struggles with literacy, especially as they move into middle school and beyond. It is a well-established fact that boys underperform on measures of literacy as compared to girls, but the reasons for their low achievement still remain debated.

According to the authors' review of research and statistics, boys take longer to learn to read than do girls, read less, and perform less well on comprehension of narrative texts and expository texts. They provide lower estimations of their reading ability, value reading less, and have less interest in leisure reading. Boys spend less time reading, enjoy it less, and are more apt to label themselves as "non-readers" (Smith & Wilhelm, 2002).

Smith and Wilhelm (2002) note that the "feminization of reading" may be one culprit, writing that "if reading or other literate activities are perceived as feminized, then boys will go to great lengths to avoid them. This is particularly true if the activities involve effort and the chance of failure, for incompetence and expending effort are also seen as unmasculine" (p. 13). Another approach to the issue may be that there simply are major differences in the way boys and girls read. This is important information for parents and educators as they support the literacy of reluctant readers.

A meta-analysis of research on gender and reading reveals some interesting differences. For example, boys tend toward informational texts, graphic novels and comic books, magazines and newspaper articles, and electronic texts more than girls do; they enjoy escapism and humor more, like to read about things they like to do (hobbies or sports), and like to collect things—therefore liking to collect series of books. They are better at information retrieval and work-related literacy activities than are girls. Boys are less likely to talk about books but prefer active responses to their reading (Smith & Wilhelm, 2002).

Jacobson (2014) suggests that one must adopt different strategies in order to entice boys to read. These include using the kinds of readings that boys value and enjoy, demonstrating the utility of what they are reading, and involving their fathers or other valued male figures or role models in literacy activities.

USING BOOKS AS THERAPY

Beyond the tensions between males and traditional reading experiences, Tatum (2005) also addresses the issue of racial identity and reading achievement. He notes that males of color—specifically Black males, in this particular book—are especially far behind in their literacy development by the time they reach middle and high school. In part, this may be for the same reasons that Smith and Wilhelm cite for males in general: the lack of perceived immediate application to "real life" and the emphasis of literary themes and information that seems to have no value in their worlds outside of the classroom.

For educators, Tatum (2005) notes the following:

Effective teachers of black males understand that they
must go beyond reading instruction. They understand,
as my own teachers did, that focusing only on skills
and strategies does little to address the turmoil that
black youths experience in America, and it may do little
to improve their reading achievement. My teachers
understood that my life experiences and how I
responded to these experiences mattered. They understood
that the texts that they placed before me had to address
some of the psychological and emotional scarring that
results from the day to day experiences. (p. 25)

This insightful advice can be extended to teachers of any students experiencing "psychological and emotional" scarring. The use of appropriate reading experiences as "bibliotherapy" has been integrated into counseling and culturally responsive pedagogy. In fact, Tatum (2005) believes that skillful teachers need to integrate readings from such fields as education, sociology, psychology, anthropology, and social work into their instruction.

The same can be true for family and community reading. The right reading choices can help children through experiences, from the loss of a beloved family member or pet to the preparation for adolescence or high school. Reading also can normalize some of the aspects of having a disability, such as anxiety or depression.

As far back as the 1950s, educators argued for the effectiveness of using books to help people understand their problems, saying, "It allows the reader to identify with a character and realize that he or she is not the only person with a particular problem. As the character works through a problem, the reader is emotionally involved in the struggle and ultimate achieves insight about his or her own situation" (Shrodes, 1955, p. 24). This can be particularly powerful for children and adolescents feeling isolated or struggling because of a learning disability.

This approach clearly can be used outside of a strictly clinical setting. Choosing readings for a child or adolescent, or forming reading groups around particular books or topics of developmental importance, is something that educators and parents can do. Librarians, reading specialists, and classroom teachers have valuable suggestions for each particular student. And there are wonderful resources online, such as Erin Moulton's (2014) "Bibliography for Teens," which lists quality readings that deal with autism, learning disabilities, depression, eating disorders, substance abuse, and other social, learning, and mental health topics.

VALUING VARIETY

For many, there is the belief that only "quality literature counts" when it comes to reading. Instead, it is essential that struggling readers see that all of their efforts at literacy are of value. This means that finding engaging material is paramount in enticing young people to read. Smith and Wilhelm (2002) interviewed young male readers to write their aforementioned book. As one informant said, "If it's interesting, I'll read it" (p. 149). But boys gave texts only scant time to interest them before they rejected them; for this reason, the authors noted the qualities that attracted boys to the act of reading.

Among these qualities was music as text—a favorite form of "reading" for boys; finding "ways to use music and other popular cultural materials as a bridge to developing more canonical literacies" (Smith & Wilhelm, 2002, p. 150) is a suggestion that encompasses all reluctant readers. Texts that are storied and those that are visual have high appeal. Reluctant readers also tend to like series of multiple books by the same author or involving the same characters; predictability of style and familiarity with characters can be reassuring and reduce some of the effort of confronting totally new texts.

Finding high-interest reading material is key for all reluctant readers. Scieszka (as cited in Gallagher, 2009) feels that children should be given as much freedom as possible to read what they want to read, not what adults think they should read. He also lobbies for expanding the definition of reading and stopping the demonization of other media: "Don't make computers and TV and movies the bad guy. Those things aren't going away. I think we did ourselves a disservice in the past by saying TV is bad, reading is good. It's not that cut and dried" (Scieszka, as cited in Gallagher, 2009, p. 84).

Smith and Wilhelm (2006) stress that educators and parents must rethink the definitions of literacy to be "aware of the digital literacies our students use, want to use, and often need to be able to use outside of school" (p. 168). Further, they say that "if we want literature to matter to our students as much as it matters to us, we need to find ways to integrate the study of literature with electronic and popular cultural texts. Doing so will engage students with new ways of knowing, reading, and writing that build on and expand those they already know" (p. 168). One benefit of this approach is that students can teach their parents and teachers about their "technoliteracies," showing them how they can learn best.

Both teachers and parents need to openly embrace a rapidly changing digital world, argues Alvermann (2002). While the flood of digital information into classrooms and homes may threaten the "knowledge authority" of teachers and parents, this trend is here to stay. Better to learn to be more tech savvy and enter the worlds of children and adolescents in order to engage them in the new literacies.

USING READING TO PROMOTE DEVELOPMENT

Reading well-chosen works can help students address transitions and developmental challenges. Seeing how fictitious and true characters have faced their own dilemmas can assist students of all ages in solving their own. Tu (1999) stresses that not only can literature help children understand that they are not alone in encountering problems, but it can also help teachers and family members understand and relate to students' feelings about these problems.

Family should feel free to approach librarians and teachers as their children need the guidance that books can provide. Tu (1999) argues that the literature that holds the most power to assist children through developmental passages must be well written and developmentally appropriate; honest in its portrayal of the situation; present multidimensional characters; provide problem-solving strategies; and offer the potential for controversy or avoid easy or pat solutions.

Crippen (2012) argues that reading helps children develop cultural identity, encourages creativity, and fosters social and personal development. She believes that quality children's literature can foster social development by creating characters who may express values, beliefs, or other differences other than the reader's own; this encourages children to enter into others' worldviews and accept diverse opinions and backgrounds.

The act of reading itself allows students to develop relationships with other people, encouraging greater social contact. In the cases of students whose learning disabilities impact their social skills, reading can play a didactic role, as it permits a sort of rehearsal of actions and responses at a remove, through reading and talking about what the characters should and should not do in certain social situations. Family can work with educational staff to identify gaps in social skills and particular reading experiences that could teach or bolster necessary skills and attitudes.

At-risk adolescents in Pittsburgh can take part in STRUGGLE, a member of the family of literacy projects at Community House. In this six-week program, adolescents work with adult partners in collaborative writing projects aimed at helping the students write their way through life struggle and learn problem-solving and life-planning skills with foundations in hope for the future. Students read and present their works and collaborate with their adult partners in articulating their life plans (Hull & Schultz, 2002). Again, the synergistic relationship among speaking, reading, and writing offers opportunities for human growth and development while simultaneously developing literacy skills.

Turning Reading into Action

Demonstrating the myriad ways that reading can provide the information for personal or social action is a key toward cementing its value. Vygotsky (1962) saw all learning as relational and social, saying that individuals learn best when they are addressing an issue or solving a problem that is of personal interest and importance. Once passionate topics are identified, struggling readers can be helped to use writing or other means of expression to address their concerns; reading then becomes the logical backdrop for informing themselves, so that they can write a letter to the editor, make a proposal to their school, express gratitude, or plan a family trip.

A genuine need for inquiry is a great motivation to read. It's hard to imagine a teenager who doesn't want to read a driver's manual in order to get his or her license! Reading that has a clear purpose is more likely to entice reluctant readers. This might be found in instructions, recipes, "how-to" guides, or travel brochures.

Reading can also be a vehicle for social action. Reluctant readers may be enticed to read as a way to help others. Family and students can read about various charitable organizations that promote reading in order to pick the recipient of their fund or donation drive. National nonprofits like Milk and Bookies, United through Reading, or Pajama Program help underserved students, the homeless, and veterans (Laviolette, 2016).

Using Local and Natural Resources

Since 1967, September 8 has been designated as International Literacy Day. UNESCO, the sponsor of the day, lists many ideas for community-school engagement, including service activities such as holding a book drive for charity or donating children's books to Books for Babies, or starting a reading club with an international theme. Charity drives, such as collecting used books for Better World Books, which accepts donations and gives them to those in need, can be woven into school community service requirements or Girl or Boy Scout badge activities.

Although many may not be aware of it, November 1 is National Family Literacy Day; in some communities and school districts, the entire month of November is targeted for family literacy activities. Read-a-thons, celebrity appearances, book drives, Read Them to Sleep sleepovers at school, and competitions are just a few of the ways that the day is celebrated.

Read across America Day (Dr. Seuss Day) is celebrated on March 2 (his birthday) or the closest school day to that date. Again, while each school or community is free to plan its own celebration, there are ideas and resources listed online that can facilitate such planning.

The National Center for Families Learning provides a website with ideas for keeping families engaged in literacy activities. They suggest holding a family-school reading day (or days) in which family members are invited to school to read favorite stories, learn about games and tools at such sites as ReadWriteThink.org, and brainstorm ways to stay engaged in the reading process throughout the year. The organization also notes that having books for families to take home, as well as certificates of participation, is a good incentive for the activities. Local bookstores and other businesses can be solicited to donate books and bookmarks.

Get Ready to Read offers a simple home literacy environment checklist that can help families gauge the "friendliness" of their home for supporting children's literacy. There are numerous websites that list activities to enhance family literacy. Among them are Wonderopolis, Reading Rockets, Reading Is Fundamental, and the International Library Association. The Reading Rockets site alone lists more than twenty sites devoted solely to family literacy.

Getting Involved

If local schools and communities do not offer family literacy opportunities, it is possible for families and community members to plan their own by promoting fun-filled activities based around literacy activities. For example, Scholastic offers a downloadable facilitator's guide for planning a Read and Rise Family Reading Night in which part of the program engages parents and family members in an interactive discussion about how to use everyday activities to build children's literacy skills and the other part of the program encourages families to work together to create their own original books, which they can take home with them.

Another focus for family-community involvement may be initiatives to get books into all families' hands. Little Free Library sites exist all around the world; build a model schoolhouse, fill it with books, and put it in visible locations in the community to promote book exchange. Include books for all ages and reading levels, and notify local media to spread the word (Laviolette, 2016).

A quick perusal of websites geared toward family and community involvement in literacy turns up dozens of ideas and downloadable resources to use in community literacy efforts. Drawing on local knowledge and traditions, as well as partnering with one's local agencies, school and family members can cooperate in developing the activities that make the most sense for their habitat.

Celebrating Reading Successes

To raise the status of reading and other literacy activities, schools and communities need to emphasize the celebration of reading success as much as they recognize athletic or academic achievements. This could involve local media publicizing the reading achievements of students or recognizing the efforts of reading mentors and community members who support reading efforts.

Schools can plan celebratory events. For example, Superintendent Ed Drapp greets students and their families at an annual "Book Blast & Bar-B-Que" to recognize K–8 students who have met summer reading challenges. Students, family, and community members eat, dance, and celebrate the act of reading (Tyson, 2013).

Engaging the Community and Beyond

Local businesses and organizations also may be willing partners. For example, the Queensbury, New York–based Six Flags Amusement Park, Great Escape, sponsors a summer reading challenge for local students. After students document their daily summer reading, they are eligible for a free day at the amusement park. Home Depot partners with Books and Bears and Operation Storybook to give children free books for their home libraries. Local or chain supermarkets often donate the necessities for a community reading celebration party or cookout.

Laviolette (2016) encourages business owners to see themselves as vital players in the community literacy movement. In her blog, she suggests that local businesses are excellent venues to encourage literacy through hosting author readings, book clubs, and book drives. Business owners can donate a portion of each sale to a designated nonprofit recipient, thus combining entrepreneurship with socially responsible sales.

CONCLUSION

With so many students at risk for being reluctant, nonfluent, or nonreaders, schools, families, and communities must collaborate in using proven strategies to enhance literacy, while creating new activities and traditions that are unique to their localities. Home-, school-, and community-based events and practices reinforce the goal of fluency for all. In this age of new technologies, new "technoliteracies" have been created. Teachers and parents need to embrace these novel literacies and expand their notions of reading and "literature" if they are to entice today's youth into seeing themselves as readers and finding a purpose for their reading.

The school-home connection can be a particularly powerful one. Parents need to see their roles in the reading partnership as lasting well beyond the elementary school years, although their strategies in supporting struggling readers will change. In addition to learning the specifics of their child's reading profile, family can inform teachers of valuable information about their child's interests and passions. In some cases, engagement in their children's literacy may spur parents to improve their own.

Community agencies and local businesses can initiate or support ongoing literacy activities by opening their doors to families through such activities as author readings, book drives, and book clubs. They can donate labor, money, publicity, food, or prizes to events that celebrate reading successes. Using one's agency or business to promote family literacy models socially responsible practices in school, such as community service or service learning activities that center on reading.

Modeling and providing the tools for reading success are key to winning the literacy battle. If parents want children to be readers, they must be readers themselves. If schools want skilled readers, they must embrace the new literacies and technologies that are part of students' lives. And if communities want a literate citizenry, they must put books and other materials in the hands of those who do not have them, provide interesting spaces to host literacy events, and join in the celebration that elevates reading successes to those of other activities such as athletics.

POINTS TO REMEMBER

- Addressing the literacy needs of learning disabled students and struggling or reluctant readers takes a collaboration between school, community, and family members who need to be mentors and advocates for literacy success.
- Family engagement in the reading process tends to drop off as students enter middle school; however, family members need to find alternate ways of staying involved in literacy activities with their children even as they enter adolescence.
- Parents and teachers should approach all struggling readers from a strengths-based approach, identifying, and using students' assets and interests to promote literacy efforts.
- It is necessary to broaden the definition of appropriate reading materials to include a wide variety of print and multimedia sources as a way to engage all readers.
- We must recognize the synergistic nature of reading, writing, and speaking when finding ways to address reading deficits.

REFERENCES

Alvermann, D. E. (Ed.). (2002). *Adolescents and literacies in a digital world.* New York, NY: Peter Lang.

Beers, K. (2005). *Choosing not to read: Understanding why some middle schoolers just say no.* Retrieved from pdfs.semanticscholar.org/7e44/27d14086ac6fe48d7f320acd2345789ad 511.pdf

Crippen, M. (2012). *The value of children's literature.* Retrieved from http://www.luther.edu/ oneota-reading-journal/archive/2012/the-value-of-childrens-literature/

Family Literacy (2015). *Family literacy: What is it.* Retrieved from http://literacy.kent.edu/ FamilyLiteracy/whatisit.html. Last updated November 4, 2015.

Ferlazzo, L. (2009, May 19). Parent engagement or parent involvement? *Learning First Alliance.* Retrieved from www.learningfirst.org/LarryFerlazzoParentEngagement

Gallagher, K. (2009). *Readicide: How schools are killing reading and what you can do about it.* Portland, ME: Stenhouse.

Garringer, M. & MacRae, P. (2008). *Building effective peer mentoring services: An introductory guide.* Folsom, CA: Mentoring Resource Center.

Graham, S., & Hebert, M. A. (2010). *Writing to read: Evidence for how writing can improve reading. A Carnegie Corporation time to act report.* Washington, DC: Alliance for Excellent Education.

Henderson, A. T. (2011). *Family-school-community partnerships 2.0: Collaborative strategies to advance learning.* Retrieved from http://www.nea.org/assets/docs/Family-School-Community-Partnerships-2.0.pdf

Hull, G., & Schultz, K. (Eds.). (2002). *School's out: Bridging out-of-school literacies with classroom practice.* New York, NY: Teachers College Press.

Jacobson, L. (2014). *Why boys don't read.* Retrieved from http://www.greatschools.org/ students/academic-skills/6832-why-so-many-boys-do-notread.gs

Kittle, P. (2013). *Book love: Developing depth, stamina, and passion in adolescent readers.* Portsmouth, NH: Heinemann.

Laviolette, J. (2016, September 8). Ways to give back to promote literacy [Blog post]. Retrieved from www.groupon.com/merchant/blog/ways-to-give-back-promote-literacy-business

Miller, D. (2014). *Reading in the wild.* San Francisco, CA: Jossey-Bass.

Moulton, E. (2014). Bibliography for teens: Helpful tips and recommended fiction. *School Library Journal.* Retrieved from http://www.slj.com/2014/11/teens-ya/bibliotherapy-for-teens-helpful-tips-and-recommended-fiction/#

National Endowment for the Arts. (2015). *A decade of arts engagement: Findings from the survey of public participation in the arts, 2002–2012.* Retrieved from https://www.arts.gov/ sites/default/files/2012-sppa-feb2015.pdf

PBS.org. (2002). *Misunderstood minds.* Retrieved from http://www.pbs.org/wgbh/ misunderstoodminds/reading.html

Perrin, A. (2016). *Book reading 2016.* Pew Research Center. Retrieved from http://www. pewinternet.org/2016/09/01/book-reading-2016/

Reader to Reader. (n.d.) *Read, think, share.* Retrieved from http://www.readertoreader.org/ literacy/mentoring

Scholastic & YouGov. (2014). *Kids and family reading report (5th ed.).* Retrieved from http:// www.scholastic.com/readingreport/Scholastic-KidsAndFamilyReadingReport-5thEdition. pdf?v=100

Shrodes, C. (1955). Bibliotherapy. *The Reading Teacher, 9,* 24–30.

Smith, M. W., & Wilhelm, J. D. (2002). *Reading don't fix no Chevys: Literacy in the lives of young men.* Portsmouth, NH: Heinemann.

Smith, M. W., & Wilhelm, J. D. (2006). *Going with the flow: How to engage boys (and girls) in their literacy learning.* Portsmouth, NH: Heinemann.

Spear-Swerling, L. (2006). *Vocabulary assessment and instruction for students with learning disabilities.* Retrieved from http://www.readingrockets.org/article/vocabulary-assessment-and-instruction-students-learning-disabilities

Tatum, A. (2005). *Teaching reading to Black adolescent males: Closing the achievement gap.* Portland, ME: Stenhouse.

Tracey, D., Hornery, S., Seaton, M., Craven, R. G., & Yeung, A. S. (2014). *Volunteers supporting children with reading difficulties in schools: Motives and rewards.* Retrieved from www.adi.org/journal/2014ss/TraceyEtalSpring2014.pdf

Tu, W. (1999). *Using literature to help children cope with problems.* ERIC Digest D148, #ED436008.

Tyson, K. (2013). 25 ways school can promote literacy and independent reading. Retrieved from http://www.teachthought.com/uncategorized/25-ways-schools-can-promote-literacy independent-reading/

Vygotsky, L. (1962). *Thought and language.* Cambridge, MA: MIT Press.

Wiener, H. S. (1988). *Talk with your child.* New York, NY: Viking.

About the Editors

Dr. Nicholas D. Young has worked in diverse educational roles for more than twenty-eight years, serving as a principal, special education director, graduate professor, graduate program director, graduate dean, and longtime superintendent of schools. He was named the Massachusetts Superintendent of the Year; and he completed a distinguished Fulbright program focused on the Japanese educational system through the collegiate level. He holds numerous graduate degrees including a PhD in educational administration and an EdD in educational psychology. Dr. Young is the recipient of numerous other honors and recognitions including the General Douglas MacArthur Award for distinguished civilian and military leadership and the Vice Admiral John T. Hayward Award for exemplary scholarship.

Dr. Young has served in the U.S. Army and U.S. Army Reserves combined for more than thirty-three years; and he graduated with distinction from the U.S. Air War College, the U.S. Army War College, and the U.S. Navy War College. After completing a series of senior leadership assignments in the U.S. Army Reserves as the commanding officer of the 287th Medical Company (DS), the 405th Area Support Company (DS), the 405th Combat Support Hospital, and the 399 Combat Support Hospital, Dr. Young transitioned to his current military position as a faculty instructor at the U.S. Army War College in Carlisle, Pennsylvania. He currently holds the rank of colonel.

Dr. Young is also a regular presenter at state, national, and international conferences; and he has coauthored or authored many books, book chapters, and/or articles on various topics in education, counseling, and psychology. Some of his most recent work includes *Collapsing Educational Boundaries from Preschool to PhD: Building Bridges across the Educational Spectrum* (2013) and *Learning Style Perspectives: Impact upon the Classroom* (3rd ed.,

2014). He was also a primary author for *The Power of the Professoriate: The Evolving in 21st Century Higher Education* (in press), *To Campus with Confidence: Supporting a Successful Transition to College for Students with Learning Disabilities* (in press), *Educational Entrepreneurship: Promoting Public-Private Partnerships for the 21st Century* (2015), *Beyond the Bedtime Story: Promoting Reading Development during the Middle School Years* (2015), *Betwixt and Between: Understanding and Meeting the Social and Emotional Developmental Needs of Students during the Middle School Transition Years* (2014), *Transforming Special Education Practices: A Primer for School Administrators and Policy Makers* (2012), and *Powerful Partners in Student Success: Schools, Families and Communities* (2012). He has also coauthored several children's books to include the popular series *I Am Full of Possibilities*. Dr. Young may be contacted directly at nyoung1191@aol.com.

Dr. Christine N. Michael is a more than forty-year educational veteran with a variety of professional experiences. She holds degrees from Brown University, Rhode Island College, Union Institute and University, and the University of Connecticut, where she earned a PhD in education, human development, and family relations. Her previous work has included middle and high school teaching, higher education administration, college teaching, and educational consulting. She has also been involved with Head Start, Upward Bound, national nonprofits Foundation for Excellent Schools and College for Every Student, and the federal Trio programs and has published widely on topics in education and psychology. Her most recent works include serving as a primary author on the book *To Campus with Confidence: Supporting a Successful Transition to College for Students with Learning Disabilities* (in press), *Beyond the Bedtime Story: Promoting Reading Development during the Middle School Years* (2015), *Betwixt and Between: Understanding and Meeting the Social and Emotional Development Needs of Students during the Middle School Transition Years* (2014), and *Powerful Partners in Student Success: Schools, Families and Communities* (2012). She is currently the program director of Low Residency Programs at American International College. Dr. Michael may be contacted at cnevadam@gmail.com.

Teresa Allissa Citro is the chief executive officer of Learning Disabilities Worldwide Inc. and the founder and president of Thread of Hope Inc. Ms. Citro is a graduate of Tufts New England Medical School and Northeastern University, Boston. She has coedited several books on a wide range of topics in special education and has coauthored a popular children's series, *I Am Full of Possibilities*. Furthermore, Ms. Citro is the coeditor of two peer review journals, *Learning Disabilities: A Contemporary Journal* and *Insights on Learning Disabilities: From Prevailing Theories to Validated Practices*. She is the mother of two young children, and she resides in Boston, Massachusetts. Ms. Citro may be contacted at tacitro@aol.com.

Made in the USA
Lexington, KY
15 January 2018